Four Days in 1865:

The Fall of Richmond

Published by Cadmus Marketing
A Division of Cadmus Communications Corporation

Managing Editor: Don J. Beville
Editors: Moira J. Saucer, Patrick R. Saucer and Patricia W. Nelson
Designed by: Melissa Savage and Thomas McDaniel

Printed in the United States

Library of Congress Catalogue Number 92-082733

ISBN 0-9629648-4-0

Fine Books Division
Cadmus Marketing
2901 Byrdhill Rd.
Richmond, Virginia 23261

804/264-2711

Four Days in 1865: The Fall of Richmond

by David D. Ryan

Introduction by John M. Coski

Published by Cadmus Communications Corporation

In Memory

Thomas Raymond Ryan, Jr.

Paul Davis Williams

Dodie Ryan Schow

E. Sherman Grable, Jr.

Marvin E. Garrette

Mary May

This book is made possible in part with grants from the Ethyl Corporation and the John Stewart Bryan Memorial Foundation, Inc.

Table of Contents

Acknowledgments and Author's Notes

*T*HIS book is the culmination of the support given me by my editors, Moira J. Saucer, Patrick R. Saucer and Patricia W. Nelson, fellow researchers and the many people who have given me moral support. I am particularly indebted to John M. Coski, historian of the Museum of the Confederacy, who read the manuscript for historical accuracy, wrote the introduction and offered many helpful suggestions to improve the book.

Maurice Duke, J. Earle Dunford, Jr., Welford Dunaway Taylor, Cynthia MacLeod and Mrs. Robbie Lue Pendegraph offered helpful suggestions. I also thank the staffs of the New York Public Library, Division of Rare Books and Manuscripts (Van Lew papers, Astor Lenox and Tilden Foundations), the Museum of the Confederacy, the Virginia State Library and Archives, the Virginia Historical Society, the Valentine Museum, the Richmond Public Library, the Historic Richmond Foundation, the Library of Congress, the National Archives, St. Paul's Episcopal Church and Second Presbyterian Church for their valuable help.

To Wallace Stettinius and Don J. Beville, thank you for your faith and patience.

This story is told primarily from letters, diaries and reports written by persons who lived in Richmond or passed through it during the period covered. Excerpts from diaries and letters are often used with the original spelling intact. In several instances I have dramatized scenes based on actual accounts.

David D. Ryan

Introduction

*T*O a generation of Richmonders, April 2, 1865 held the same significance that V-J Day and November 22, 1963 hold for a more recent generation of Americans. Whether they were among the worshipers in St. Paul's Episcopal Church who witnessed the summons of President Jefferson Davis or whether they heard the news secondhand, those Richmonders of more than 125 years ago always remembered where they were and what they were doing when they learned of the impending evacuation of the Confederate capital city.

The first days of April, 1865 in Richmond were as rich in drama, poignancy and irony as any in American history. April 2nd dawned bright and beautiful. It was, one woman remembered, "one of those unusually lovely days that the Spring sometimes brings." Within 24 hours the perfect spring day had become a perfect Hell on earth. "The sky in the direction of Richmond is lurid with the glare of burning houses," Kate Mason Rowland wrote in her diary on April 3d. "All day since early dawn the air has been filled with shells bursting & columns of smoke & flame ascending from the burning magazines and government buildings. . . . It was as if a great battle were going on around us. This has all been done by our own people."

Indeed, the most bitter irony for the people of Richmond was not only that the fire was set by Confederate forces but also that the dreaded "Yankees" entered the city as conquerors and saviors. Even the most patriotic Southerner credited the Federal troops with extinguishing the fires and imposing order on a city gone mad. Still, Kate Mason Rowland wrote, "I think our patriotic citizens would be willing to loose [sic] a little personal property for the sake of lessening the triumph of our foes. Better lay the whole city in ashes than give the enemy any munition of war—one drop of 'aid and comfort.'" When the shock of the evacuation and the conflagration passed, residents were left with blocks of burned-out buildings and other tangible symbols of what had occurred. "The streets fairly swarmed with blue uniforms and negroes decked in the spoils of jewelry shops, etc.," Constance Cary wrote. "It is no longer our Richmond. . . . "

The burning of Richmond was an appropriate denouement for four years of war. The surrender of the capital city and the defeat of the Confederacy had long seemed imminent—some would say inevitable—and residents had begun to resign themselves to it. But, when the event actually came to pass, it was accomplished not with resignation, but with a final fury. Fire—in Richmond, Atlanta, Columbia, South Carolina and Chambersburg, Pennsylvania—had become a common fate for cities in a war that was at times anything but civil.

Four Days in 1865 dramatizes the inherently dramatic events in Richmond in April, 1865. Based on documentary research, it uses letters, diaries and reminiscences to tell the story of the Confederate evacuation and federal occupation of Richmond. David Ryan blends the techniques of historical narrative with those of fiction to give voice and texture to eyewitness accounts. The result is a sweeping portrait of events rich in symbolism for the city of Richmond, the Southern Confederacy, and for the American Civil War.

John M. Coski
Staff Historian
Museum of the Confederacy

Sunday, April 2

*B*ELOW Church Hill two- and three-story wood and brick homes line Shockoe Valley for a quarter-mile to the foot of the steep Broad Street hill. The valley is cut by a meandering stream from which it takes its name. Church spires rise from the crest of the opposite hill, but the most prominent building is the Greek Revival Capitol designed by Thomas Jefferson.

To the south of the Capitol stand rows of tobacco warehouses and flour mills along the north bank of the James River. Two railroad bridges and one passenger and vehicle bridge cross the river from the city to the town of Manchester on the south bank.

About 25 miles to the south of this capital of the Confederacy, the Army of Northern Virginia has been fighting at Petersburg against overwhelming numbers of Union soldiers to halt the march on Richmond, the capture of which has been the goal for the Union Army for four years. Muffled sounds like distant thunder could be heard all day yesterday, but it is quiet today.

1

*We have vague and incoherent accounts from
excited couriers of fighting, without result, in
Dinwiddie County, near the South Side Railroad.
It is rumored that a battle will probably occur
in that vicinity to-day.*
           —JOHN BEAUCHAMP JONES[1]

*T*HE Confederate messenger left the War Department building across from Capitol Square and began walking up Shockoe Hill. The street was bathed in morning sunlight. Only a few other persons were visible—small groups of citizens clustered at the War Department and other government buildings, hoping for news on the latest battles. An order for a news blackout had been issued several weeks before, and the messenger ignored their questions. Most Richmonders were now in church.

The trees lining Capitol Square were showing tiny new leaves and the smell of wild onions came from the hills sloping down from the Capitol building. The annual rite of nature's renewal had begun, but there was a sense of impending disaster in the air.

The messenger walked a block and a half up the hill to Grace Street, where St. Paul's Episcopal Church stood at the southwest corner. The church's grayish-white, needle-pointed spire rose prominently on the skyline. The congregation this day consisted of many women dressed in black, who were mourning fathers, sons and brothers killed in battle. The males were mostly government officials, soldiers on leave or convalescing and citizens too old or too young to be in the army. Many of the older men made up the local defense force.

One pew, No. 111, was empty. It was reserved for General Robert E. Lee, commander of the Army of Northern Virginia, and his family.

Shafts of sunlight spilled through the east-facing windows and brightened the white interior walls and columns. The members and guests sat in 104 pews on the lower level and two rows of pews in the gallery flanking each side of the church.

Halfway up the right side of the first floor in pew No. 63 sat a slim man with a goatee. He was dressed in Confederate gray trousers and vest and a gray Prince Albert coat. A wide-brimmed gray hat lay on the seat beside him. The black wavy hair on his uncovered head curled around his ears and neck. His deep-set eyes were transfixed on Dr. Charles G. Minnigerode, but the man had difficulty concentrating on the rector's words. As long as there were Southerners willing to fight, the Confederacy would live on, he reasoned. Should Virginia fall to the Yankees, the Confederate government could move farther south and function there, maybe in Louisiana. Some in the congregation said silent prayers for this man, for he was under stresses that caused his shoulders to droop. Others looked upon him as a failure. That his wife and family were not with him drew little attention, for most of the parishioners knew they had left the city several days before with the man's secretary, Burton Harrison, for a safe city farther south.*

As the rector began his communion sermon, the messenger climbed the eight steps of the church's front entrance and slipped quietly through one of the side doors. He stopped at the two large doors that opened into the sanctuary and peeked through a crack. The area of view was too small, so he walked to the two wooden doors to the left and scanned the church through a window in one door. The object of his search was standing in the back to the left of the doors, a large man dressed in a faded gray coat with brass buttons. Ruffles hung from the bosom and waist of his shirt.

This was the domain of Sexton William Irving. Sunday was his favorite day. Like an orchestra conductor, he possessed the power to make the service successful. His role was to direct, to lead the prominent citizens to their pews, to keep the service moving and to keep the younger members of the congregation in check.

The sexton rocked on his heels as he scanned the church for any event which would require his personal attention. The rector's words were but a distant noise to his ears. The movement at the side door caught his attention, and he turned to see the messenger motioning to him. Irving stepped to the door. The messenger tilted his head towards the middle of

---

*Unknown to the man, his family had not yet reached the safe house in Charlotte, N.C., but was stranded on a train in a leaky coach full of vermin.

the church and handed the sexton a folded telegram. Irving nodded.

The sexton walked slowly up the aisle, his body erect and stately. Young Dallas Tucker leaned on the railing in the gallery above, twisting a button on his shirt. He raised his head and turned toward the back of the church, and his eyes followed the sexton down the aisle.

Irving stopped at pew No. 63, bent over and whispered in the ear of the seated gentleman while handing him the telegram. The man nodded, expressionless. The rector asked for the parishioners to pray with him. The congregation moved forward as one body and knelt. Only then did the man rise quietly, take his hat and begin to walk slowly to the back of the church. He placed the felt hat on his head and stepped outside. Withdrawing the telegram from his inside coat pocket, he read it.[2]

Petersburg, April 2, 1865
His Excellency, President Davis, Richmond Va.:
   I think it is absolutely necessary that we should abandon our position tonight. I have given all the necessary orders on the subject to the troops, and the operation, though difficult, I hope will be performed successfully. I have directed General Stevens* to send an officer to Your Excellency to explain the routes to you by which the troops will be moved to Amelia Court House, and furnished you with a guide and any assistance that you may require for yourself.

R.E. Lee[3]

The president re-pocketed the telegram, his face showing little emotion. He had known the fall of Richmond was coming. Preparations had been made a year ago to remove the government to some other city should the situation in Richmond become untenable. The time had now come.

2

Within minutes of Davis's departure, further messages were brought to the sexton. One government official after another rose from his pew and left the church. The parishioners became

---

*General Walter H. Stevens

uneasy and began to whisper to each other. Dr. Minnigerode had difficulty holding the attention of his charges. Then he was called from the altar.

This excitement became manifest . . . . When the sexton appeared the fourth time, Dallas Tucker would later write, all restraint of place and occasion yielded. Good Dr. Minnigerode, he might just as well have tried to turn back the waters of Niagara Falls.[4]

"The provost marshal wants to see you in the vestry," Dr. Minnigerode's assistant whispered. The rector quickly took the 20 strides to the vestry room where he found Major Isaac Carrington waiting. The major informed him that General Lee's lines had broken at Petersburg and that a retreat had been ordered. He instructed Dr. Minnigerode to tell members of the home guard to report to the Capitol at three o'clock for instructions.

Grim-faced, the rector hurried back to the sanctuary where he found many in the congregation heading for the exits. He pleaded for them to stay for the completion of the celebration.

Those who remained in the church resumed their seats and a small number of those at the outside door returned. The service continued with about 250 members present. As they stood for the final blessing, most hung their heads in reverence, but their shoulders also slumped from the black depression spreading through the church.[5]

3

Four blocks west of St. Paul's, Dr. Moses D. Hoge also faced a sober and anxious congregation at Second Presbyterian Church. A tall, dignified man in his forties with a dark moody brow, Hoge was renowned as an orator. His "voice ranged from aeolian to thunder." So well-known were his sermons that two years earlier Queen Victoria had commanded him to preach "in the royal presence."[6]

Dr. Hoge placed his hands on each side of the dark wood pulpit and raised his eyes to the ceiling, where the arching mahogany-colored hardwood beams absorbed the little light let in by the 14 windows. The darkness of the church interior seemed to accentuate the gloom now descending on the congregation. Dr. Hoge began to pray.

"Heavenly Father, watch over our beloved city today. Guide us, particularly those in our government and our valiant soldiers on the battlefields who are fighting the evil oppression sweeping down upon us . . . . "

Dr. Hoge paused. Then in a low voice he told the people that he was torn as to what course of action to pursue. His heart told him to stay with them, but his mind said he must be with the president. As long as the Confederate Army was fighting, he must be with the men and their leader.

The parishioners stirred at these remarks and many began to whisper. Was this a farewell speech? Were the rumors that President Davis was leaving Richmond true? Was Dr. Hoge telling them he was leaving with the president? As if to confirm their questions, another messenger came up the aisle, bent over and whispered to a Confederate officer. The officer got up and left with the messenger.

Dr. Hoge looked from person to person. He held up his hand to quiet the members and then asked them to bow their heads.

"With lowly reverence of spirit, and hearts filled with sadness and awe, we come into Thy presence, Oh God, most high and holy. We come to humble ourselves under Thy mighty hand; to acknowledge that clouds and darkness surround Thee; that we cannot measure the depths of Thy infinite decrees, or fathom the wisdom of Thy inscrutable providences.

"Enable us then to feel our helplessness, our ignorance, our frailty. When we cannot explain the reasons of Thy dispensations, may we be silent; when we cannot comprehend, may we adore!

"Amen!"[7]

Dr. Hoge then announced his receipt of distressing news. General Lee's lines had broken at Petersburg and the beloved commander was evacuating his army. He could not bring himself to use the word "retreating."

As the congregation sat dumbfounded, Dr. Hoge walked slowly and deliberately down from the pulpit to the center of the altar. He took up the songbook and motioned with his hand for the congregation to rise. The organist began the introduction to the "Doxology to Old Hundredth."

Dr. Hoge's voice rang out above the music. The congregation, still in shock, sang the first line without heart. The minister's voice thundered and by the second line the congregation's voices had taken up the song. The church was filled with singing that carried beyond the wood rafters, windows and brick walls to passersby.

4

Judith W. McGuire was attending St. James's Episcopal Church on Franklin Street when messages began to arrive by couriers and Confederate officers who received them left the service. After church her children joined her for their traditional Sunday gathering.

> . . . *After the salutations of the morning, J. remarked, in an agitated voice, to his father, that he had just returned from the War Department, and that there was sad news— General Lee's lines had been broken, and the city would probably be evacuated within twenty-four hours. Not until then did I observe that every countenance was wild with excitement. . . . We could do nothing; no one suggested any thing to be done. We reached home with a strange, unrealizing feeling. In an hour J. . . . received orders to accompany Captain [William H.] Parker. . . . with the Corps of Midshipmen. Then we began to understand that the Government was moving, and that the evacuation was indeed going on.*[8]

5

Mrs. W. W. Crump tightened the strings to her bonnet and walked down the steps of St. Paul's Church. Her children joined her—Emmie, 17, Fanny, 15, Beverley, 13, Edward, 10 and their cousin Kate Tabb, 16, from Mathews County. The family trooped across Ninth Street and into Capitol Square. Beverley and Edward ran off to circle the Capitol. Mrs. Crump started to protest, but decided it would be a waste of energy. The boys had done this every Sunday when the family returned to their home at Twelfth and Broad streets.

6

Lt. General Richard S. Ewell, "Old Bald Head," paced back and forth in his office. General Lee had transferred Ewell to command the Richmond defenses after Ewell had fallen from his horse at Spotsylvania. Since the fall had made him unfit for further field service, he was dispatched to head the defense of the city. There had been little time to rest since.

Lt. General Ewell wrestled now with the problems before him—how to move Custis Lee's artillery? How to feed the soldiers who had been going one, even two days without food?

An aide asked if there were any orders. Ewell had already pondered this question. There had been correspondence with General Lee, and decisions had been made a month earlier. He ordered the aide to begin the evacuation of prisoners; to turn the storehouses open; to move supplies to the railroad depot and then to let the citizens take the remainder. He paused and looked out the window. The tobacco warehouses would be taken care of tonight, he said.[9]

General Ewell started to speak further but was interrupted by a woman's demand to see him. The family's horse had been taken by the soldiers, he heard her say. Ewell motioned for his aide to bring in the woman. She was dressed in a purple, ankle-length dress. One of "his men," she told the general, had stolen "George," the family's carriage horse. The woman cried that the children were devastated; that the horse was like a member of the family.

Ewell relaxed his military composure. He took the woman's hand and comforted her. It had been his fault, he explained. He had ordered every horse rounded up to move supplies to the Danville Depot. The children would have their horse back, he promised. Ewell told his aide to accompany the woman to the depot and to retrieve the horse.[10]

7

Chimborazo Hospital stood at the east end of Broad Street, sprawling across one of the highest hill crests in the city. The site had a commanding view of Rocketts Landing and the bend in the James River. A few ships of the tiny Confederate Navy lay at anchor across the river. The hospital complex consisted of seven rows of white frame buildings totaling more than 100 in number. The hospital could house 8,000 patients and over 77,000 had been treated there during the war.

The census now, however, was relatively low. Many of the remaining sick and wounded, even "hospital rats," who feigned sickness to escape the fighting, had left in fear of the near-certain invasion by the enemy. Rumors that the government was preparing to leave Richmond passed among the patients almost daily.

Thus it was that Phoebe Yates Pember, the hospital matron, found her workload had finally slackened for the first time in the three years of her tenure at the facility. Educated at a Northern finishing school, Mrs. Pember had taken a position previously filled only by males. Prejudice against this Georgian woman had persisted since.

"'Well' said a poor wounded fellow when told by the ward attendant that I was matron of the hospital," Mrs. Pember wrote in her diary. "'I always did think this government was a confounded sell [sic] and now I am sure of it, when they put such a little fool to manage such a big hospital at this.'"

For anyone to take Phoebe Pember for a fool would have been a mistake. Many a patient and jealous staff member had soon found this 39-year-old widow to be as strong-willed as the best of men. Even some of the doctors retreated when they found out what a tiger she was. Mrs. Pember was stern, yet compassionate. The blood and pain of the crude amputations and operations turned her stomach, but the patients could never tell from her expression. Amputations were carried out almost continuously, many times without anesthetics. Chloroform was nearly always in short supply because of the Union blockade of Southern ports.

Mrs. Pember squeezed their hands as the patients gritted their teeth. The sound of the saw cutting through the bones and the blood spurting across the sheets caused many women volunteers and even a few male aides to faint. Not Phoebe. After operations, she carried severed legs and arms and placed them outside the operating room for disposal. Time and again she came back to hold the hand of a boy who would lose his limb because gangrene had set in before the amputation.

As Mrs. Pember went about her morning tour of the buildings, she paused at a wooden-legged cot that lay empty. Sitting down, she recalled when the bed was occupied by a soldier from her home state.

"Kin you writ me a letter?" the soldier asked.

He was a woodsy looking lad, lean, yellow-complexioned with strands of hair hanging over his thin cheekbones. Others referred to him as a "Goober." She sat down on his cot and took a pen and paper from her dress pocket.

"Why do you not let the nurse cut your nails?" she asked.

"Because I ain't got any spoon, and I use them instead."

The nails were so long they had begun to curl at the ends like claws.

"Will you let me have your hair cut . . . ?"

"No. I can't . . . , kase as how I promised my mammy . . . . It's unlucky to cut it."

"Then I can't write any letter for you."

The soldier considered the predicament.

"If you writ my letter, I'll let my hair be cut and nails clipped."

"My Dear Mammy," the Goober began.

I hope this finds you well, as it leaves me well, and I hope that I shall git a furlough Christmas, and come and see you, and I hope you will keep well, and all the folks be well by that time, as I hopes to be well myself. . . .

The soldier continued in a confused circle of thoughts.

She paused and asked him a few questions about his home, his position during the last summer's campaign, how he got sick and where his brigade was at that time. This furnished some material to work upon; the letter proceeded rapidly. Four sides were conscientiously filled, for no soldier would think a letter worth sending home that showed any blank paper.

"Did you write all that?" the Goober asked.

"Yes."

"Did I say all that?"

"I think you did."

There was a pause and then the soldier asked:

"Are you married?"

"I am not. At least I am a widow."

He rose higher in bed. He pushed away the tangled hair on his brow. A faint color fluttered over the hollow cheeks and he stretched out a long piece of bone with a talon attached and gently touched her arm.

"You wait!" he whispered.[11]

8

President Davis walked down Shockoe Hill from St. Paul's Church. Rarely showing emotion during crises, he was nevertheless distracted. He barely acknowledged those who passed him. There were now many people on the streets. Horse-drawn wagons with government supplies sped up and down the hill. Government workers carried boxes of Confederate records from buildings and piled them on the sidewalks. There was shouting. Small groups of citizens gathered near the War Department. The noontime was charged with an atmosphere of uncertainty and fear.

Davis calmly reviewed the comments he would make to his cabinet. This would perhaps be their last meeting in the southern capital.

The president crossed Ninth Street and walked along Bank Street at the bottom of Capitol Square. At Tenth he turned south, walked to Main Street and turned east. He paused for a moment to look around. Soldiers on horse and foot—many in threadbare uniforms—and citizens had filled the street. Businessmen ran in and out of their stores and offices carrying armloads of valuables. Davis turned and walked up the granite steps of the Customs House, a three-story, Italianate-style building. It had been built two years before the war by the federal government. The first floor housed the Confederate Treasury Department. Its halls were filled with boxes as staff personnel prepared to move to the Danville Depot.

The president took the steps to his third floor office. Waiting for him was Navy Secretary Stephen Mallory, who had come directly from 11 o'clock Mass at the Roman Catholic Cathedral at Eighth and Grace streets.[12] The secretary reported hearing that Mr. Davis had "fled the city."

At Mallory's comments the tension in the president's face suddenly drained. He broke into laughter. A staff officer passing the president's office stopped, startled. He had not heard his commander in chief laugh for some time. Davis and Mallory left the office and walked up the street to the War Department.

An aide opened the eight-foot-high oak doors to the conference room for the two men. Soon joining them was the stout, dark, and immaculate Judah P. Benjamin, puffing on his usual Havana cigar and holding a slender gold-headed cane. The secretary of state showed no outward signs of stress despite the impending fall of Richmond; rather he was his usual "devil may care" self. Postmaster General John H. Reagan, the brisk, demanding and unpolished Texan, barely nodded to the others as he entered and sat down heavily in a chair. He was still angry at being brushed off by the president when he tried to deliver a telegram from General Lee to Davis as the president was on the way to church.

Treasury Secretary George Alfred Trenholm slumped in his chair, resting his pale face on one hand. He wheezed and coughed from his latest illness. Among the observers invited to the meeting were Virginia Governor William "Extra Billy" Smith, the aging Richmond Mayor Joseph Mayo and former Virginia Governor John Letcher, a Davis confidant.

The president stood to address those present. He had sent a telegram to General Lee, he said, asking Lee to hold Petersburg. But the general had responded that the breaks in the defense lines could not be restored. The primary escape route from Richmond was under fire. The Richmond & Petersburg Railroad line could not be used. The alternative escape route along the Richmond and Danville tracks would not remain open long.

He directed cabinet members to join other government officials in packing up and moving. They would leave tonight and go by train to Danville, where the government would set up new headquarters. The cabinet would reconvene there the following morning.

As the cabinet members hurried out, Mayor Mayo stopped at Davis's side and asked about plans to protect the citizens left in Richmond. Davis gave the mayor an irritated look and told him to see General Ewell for instructions. The president left the building and began the five-block walk to the Confederate White House.

9

John Leyburn turned up Franklin Street at Eighth and glanced at the three-story brick house on the south side. The curtains were closed over the windows of General Lee's house. The general's wife, Mary Custis Lee, had not been seen for days and he had heard she was ill. Leyburn turned his head away from the house. He did not wish to give the appearance of staring.

The nearest Leyburn had come to combat had been May 15,

1862. He had gone with other Richmonders to watch a battle at Drewry's Bluff, eight miles below the capital on the James River. Several Union ships had exchanged fire with Confederate cannons situated high on the bluff. The Union fire failed to damage the Rebel fort, but the Confederate cannons had damaged the ships. The presence of the enemy so close to the city had left its inhabitants shaken. So had General George B. McClellan's campaign in the spring and summer of that year, even though he was decisively defeated by General Lee in the Seven Days' Battles. During General Philip Sheridan's raid on Richmond last May in which the popular Confederate General J.E.B. Stuart was killed, Richmonders could hear the sound of the cannon fire. Sheridan was stopped north of the city at Yellow Tavern by Confederate General Wade Hampton. Now the Union armies were at the gates of the city.

Leyburn stopped in front of a two-story brick house a block away from the Lee house. He adjusted his coat and knocked on the door. A woman opened the door cautiously, invited him inside, and then glanced out to check the street. The last time she had ventured to look, it was practically empty. Now the street was bursting with people hurrying to reach their destinations.

Leyburn entered the parlor, where two other women were waiting. One asked him what news he had heard. A Presbyterian minister himself, Leyburn reported hearing that near chaos had marked the ending of the service at St. Paul's. The women gasped. The president had been called out of the service and General Joseph R. Anderson of the Tredegar Iron Works left soon after, Leyburn reported. He told the women that it was rumored that Davis, the government people and the military were to leave the city that night.

"What will happen to us?" cried one of the women.

Her daughter expressed fears of being raped by Yankees, but Leyburn assured them that it was doubtful they would be molested by the Union soldiers. If he were a woman, he said, he would worry more about their own soldiers, those who desert and stay behind. They might rob and steal or even rape, and with the government gone, he also had concern that the prisoners at the penitentiary might escape.

The three women began to wail, holding onto each other and rocking back and forth until Leyburn shouted for them to stop and do something to protect their valuable property. At his direction the women began to gather silverware, bracelets, watches, necklaces and knickknacks. He suggested they sew pockets in their petticoats to hide the items, and the women took to the work in an almost festive manner.[13]

10

Virginia Dare had missed attending church because she was nursing her ill sister at the boardinghouse where they lived. She joined the unfolding drama when she opened the front door, eagerly seeking reports of the war.

> *. . . about the time I supposed the congregation would be dispersing from their various places of worship, I stepped to the door to inquire from any passing acquaintance the news from "the front."*
>
> *The first person I saw at the door was a fellow lodger, Miss Bowers, who came tottering up the steps, pale and agitated, exclaiming: "Oh! have you heard the dreadful news? General Lee's right flank has given away; he has been compelled to retreat, and Richmond is to be evacuated immediately! While Dr. Hoge was in the midst of his sermon a messenger came hurriedly into the church, walked up the aisle, handed him a note and quickly left. Dr. Hoge glanced anxiously over the mysterious paper, bowed his head for a moment in silence on his desk, then rising said: 'Brethren, trying scenes are before us. General Lee has been defeated; but remember that God is with us in the storm as well as the calm'. . ."*
>
> *Next came Mrs. Porter from St. Paul's Church crying, "Oh! Miss Lucy, have you heard that the city is to be evacuated immediately and the Yankees will be here before morning? . . . What can it all mean? And what is to become of us poor defenceless women, God only knows!"*[14]

11

After the service at St. Paul's, a woman sought safety from the encroaching chaos by returning to her room at the Spottswood* Hotel at the southeast corner of Eighth and Main streets. Later, using the name "Agnes," to keep her identity secret, she wrote about her experiences to her friend, Mrs. Robert A. Pryor, in Petersburg.

As soon as I reached the hotel I wrote a note to the proprietor, asking for news. He answered that grave tidings had come from Petersburg, and for himself he was by no means sure we could hold Richmond. He requested me to keep quiet and not encourage a tendency to excitement or panic. At first I thought I would read my services in the quiet of my little sky parlor at the Spotswood, but I was literally in a fever of anxiety. I descended to the parlor. Nobody was there except two or three children. Later . . . I walked out and met Mr. James Lyons.† He said there was no use in further evading the truth. The lines were broken at Petersburg and that town and Richmond would be surrendered. . . .

I asked Judge Lyons what we would do.

"I shall stand my ground. I have a sick family, and we must take our chances together."

"Then seriously—really and truly—Richmond is to be given up, after all, to the enemy?"

"Nothing less! And we are going to have a rough time. I imagine."

I could not be satisfied until I had seen Judge Campbell,‡ upon whom we so much relied for good, calm sense. I found him with his hands full of papers, which he waved deprecatingly as I entered [his office].

"Just a minute, Judge! I am alone at the Spotswood and—"

"Stay here [in the city], my dear lady! You will be perfectly safe. I advise all families to remain in their own houses. Keep quiet. . . . "

With this advice I returned and mightily reassured and comforted the proprietor of the Spotswood. He immediately caused notice to be issued to the guests . . . .[15]

---

*Also spelt Spotswood in some accounts.

†Judge James Lyons lived north of Richmond at "Laburnum" on the Brook Turnpike.

‡Judge John A. Campbell.

2

*T*HE Confederate president climbed the seven marble steps to the front porch of the executive mansion. He pushed open the right of the two wooden front doors and handed his hat to his manservant, James Jones. The weary president turned to his right and climbed the circular staircase. Once upstairs he walked slowly across the hallway and turned right into his office. He sat down heavily in his chair behind his cherry desk.

He dropped his head into his long, bony hands. For nearly a minute he rested his head and then slowly raised it. The stone public mask that rarely left his face was gone, replaced by an expression of exhaustion. Deep furrows ran across his forehead, darkened by shadows rendered by the sunlight filtering through the window curtains.

He reached over and grasped a small framed photograph of his wife, Varina. It showed a beautiful, dark-haired woman, 18 years his junior, in a full-length, purple satin dress. Her long black hair was clasped behind her head. The dress lay off her shoulders and crossed in a curving V across her breast. He also fingered individual portraits of his children—Margaret, the eldest, her hair drifting across the shoulders of her neck-high dress; the youngest, Varina Anne; William, three and a half, and Jefferson, Jr., eight. There had been two other children who had died in youth, Samuel Emory at the age of two, and Joseph Evan "Little Joe," who died at the age of five.

Davis recalled his first meeting with Varina on the porch of "Diamond Place," a Mississippi plantation. She was so young and so beautiful, her dark hair heightened by the white dress she wore. The years between them had caused Varina concern. "I do not know whether this Mr. Jefferson Davis is young or old. He looks both at times, but I believe he is old . . .," she had written after their first meeting.[1]

The two were married in 1845, 10 years after the death of Davis's first wife, Sarah Knox Taylor. Both Davis and she had caught malaria on their honeymoon. She had died and the fever periodically returned in Davis.

A soft knock at the door broke the president's trance. The manservant, Jones, entered and asked his chief if he were ready. The two men walked into the adjacent master bedroom. The manservant set a valise and a small dressing case on the four-poster bed and began to take a few articles from the armoire. He also placed in the case a few of the president's toiletries from the dressing table.

In the valise the president placed four pistols and some ammunition. One pistol was an 1851 Colt Navy six-shot revolver with an eight-inch barrel. Another was the two-barreled Stuadenmeyer he had used in the Indian and Mexican Wars. Lastly he placed into the valise two photographs.

The president walked back through his office and opened a door to the east side of the second floor. The door led to a nursery extending the length of the house. Along the back wall were a small bed and a crib used by Margaret and Varina Anne, respectively. One adult-sized and three child-sized rocking chairs rested in the center of the room. In front of the chairs was a toy iron cannon modeled after those placed along the city's defense lines. At the head of the room was a bed used by Mrs. Davis when her husband was out of town or working late. At the foot of her bed was another crib. The sight of the empty nursery brought thoughts of his son, "Little Joe."[2]

> *Near the end of April 1864 the city was threatened from all sides by Yankee troops. The president had been sleeping little and he often forgot to eat. Mrs. Davis had begun to take him a basket of food to his office each day. On the last day of the month, she left the children playing in the nursery, prepared the food and carried it to him. As she lifted the towel from the basket, a servant ran into the room.*
>
> *"Little Joe is hurt. Lord! I think he killed himself!"*
>
> *"What?" screamed Mrs. Davis. "Where is he?"*
>
> *"Outside in back. Oh, Mr. President, it wasn't my fault," the Irish nurse cried hysterically.*
>
> *The Davises ran down the stairs and out to the yard. Lying crumpled on the brick walk below the porch was Little Joe. His older brother, Jeff, knelt over him sobbing.*
>
> *"I have said all the prayers I know how, but God will not wake Joe," cried Jeff.*
>
> *The president knelt down beside his two sons. He raised Jeff and guided him to his mother. Gently, he cradled*

Little Joe in his arms and carried him into the house. His little joy and hope lay limp in his arms, recalled family friend and diarist Mary Chesnut. Before Mrs. Chesnut left the house that evening, she saw Joe lying in the bed, "white and beautiful as an angel, covered with flowers. Catherine, his nurse, was flat on the floor by his side, weeping and wailing as only an Irishwoman can."
Davis uttered, "Not mine, O Lord, but thine."[3]

The president looked away from the crib and then walked slowly from the nursery. He softly closed the door. At the bottom of the staircase, he paused, changed his mind about going into the entrance hall, and walked instead into the small study where he and Varina sometimes read together. A small table was still set for tea. He fondled one of the cups and then walked into the drawing room. The high walls were decorated in burgundy-colored wallpaper, as was the adjacent parlor. On many nights the family gathered in that room to read the Bible and on other nights both the parlor and the drawing room were filled with guests.

Of the couple, Varina was the extrovert. She welcomed opportunities for social gatherings as a release from the tensions of the war. When she entered the room the gathering came alive with laughter and loud talk. For a visitor she might relate odd experiences of her public life with descriptions and flashes of humor. She discussed the latest book or talked knowingly of opera.

Mr. Davis spoke little during the social events, seeming to prefer to sit back and enjoy his wife's conversation. Occasionally he clinched an argument or provided an opinion that quickly settled a contention. One night a burly boisterous guest from South Carolina commented for all to hear:

"Every Southerner is equal to three Yankees at least."

Other guests laughed and raised their glasses to the comment, except for the president. He sat his glass down and turned towards the man.

"Sir! It will be a long war. Only fools doubt the courage of the Yankees."

The Carolinian's mouth fell open, and he spoke little more for the remainder of the evening.[4]

The president passed through the parlor door and into the

entrance hall. Mrs. O'Melia handed him his hat. He covered his head and then took her hand and said softly: "Treat the Union commander as you would any of our guests."

"Yes, Mr. President."

Davis walked down the porch steps. His manservant was waiting with the president's horse, "Kentucky."

2

Secretary of State Benjamin worked feverishly to pack his personal papers. His usual cool, meticulous demeanor wavered. He did not notice his friend, Alfred Paul, observing him from the door. The French consul was surprised at what he saw.

"I found him extremely agitated," he would later write to the French Ministry in Paris. "His hands shaking, wanting and trying to do and say everything at once. He was preparing to leave at five o'clock with the President and his other colleagues."[5]

Benjamin looked up and saw Paul. He took a deep breath to compose himself and greeted the consul. The men shook hands. Benjamin reminded M. Paul that the consul had predicted this day after the Union victory at Gettysburg. Yes, the consul remembered, but he said he was sorry for Benjamin's sake and his other Southern friends to see it finally arrive.

For a few moments the two men stood in embarrassed silence. Would the consul be staying? Benjamin inquired. No, M. Paul said, he would go to Washington. The Confederate government was going to Danville, Benjamin noted. Perhaps they would meet again soon. Finally M. Paul grabbed Benjamin by the shoulders and kissed him on both cheeks.

"God watch over you, Judah."[6]

3

Below the city Raphael H. Semmes was sitting down to lunch in his cabin aboard his flagship, *Virginia II*. A handsome man in his thirties, the admiral twisted his moustache while awaiting his lunch. Sheltered by the heavy walls of his cabin, he was ignorant of the upheaval in the nearby city.

The table was set with pewter dinnerware. A cotton napkin was alongside his fork. He unfolded the napkin and placed it in his lap. There was a knock at the door, and he commanded the visitor to enter. Instead of the Admiral's lunch the sailor held an envelope. Surprised, he stood up and took it, then sat back down. His face went pale as he opened the envelope and read the enclosed message.

Sir:
General Lee advises the Government to withdraw from this city, and the officers will leave this evening accordingly. I presume that General Lee has advised you of this, and of his movements, and made suggestions as to the disposition to be made of your squadron . . . Let your people be rationed as far as possible for the march, and armed and equipped for duty in the field.
Very respectfully, your obedient servant,
S.R. Mallory, Secretary of the Navy[7]

Semmes pushed back his chair, put down his napkin and observed, "This is short notice. Why wasn't I told before?" He dismissed the sailor, and walked to the porthole. As he looked across the river at the city, his thoughts focused on the peaceful scene before him.

The sun was shining brightly, the afternoon was calm, and nature was just beginning to put on her spring attire. The fields were green with early grass, the birds were beginning to twitter, and the plowman has already broken up his fields for planting his corn. I look abroad upon the landscape and contrast the peace and quiet of nature, so heedless of man's woes, with the disruption of a great Government and the ruin of an entire people which were at hand![8]

The chugging sound of a boat engine interrupted his thoughts. Semmes stepped to the side and peered downriver through the porthole. A boat flying a flag of truce made its way towards his ship. The truce boat was crowded beyond capacity with Confederate prisoners freed at Drewry's Bluff. The boat passed his ship, and the prisoners broke into enthusiastic cheering at the sight of the Confederate flag flying from her mast.

"Poor devils. If only they knew," Semmes thought.

4

Rebecca Jane Allen and two of her sons watched from Chimborazo Hill as the Confederate prisoners disembarked from the truce boat at Rocketts Landing below. The cheers of the former prisoners and the shouts of joy from their relatives drifted up. The youngest boy asked his mother if his father were among the released prisoners. These were men captured by the Yankees, she explained. His father was still fighting with General Lee.

They watched until the last prisoners had come ashore and then began the walk back to their house on Main Street. The winter pallor of Rebecca's face was accentuated by her long red hair. She was slightly plump from eating too many potatoes, about the only substantial food the family could afford. She missed her husband. Some nights she was in tears from worry and fear over his safety and her uncertain ability to provide for the two boys. Somehow, however, she bore the burden, as did so many other women in the same predicament.[9]

5

Despite warnings, Emmie Crump set out for a Sunday school class she helped with at a black church. As she walked up the north side of Broad Street, she heard repeated shouts that the Yankees were coming. People ran back and forth across the wide, dirt street kicking up dust; men carried baggage and trunks on their shoulders, dodging horses and wagons. The noise was frightening. Turning north on Twelfth Street, she heard her name called out. Looking back, she saw a friend from St. Paul's Church, a young woman her own age. Her friend told her to return home. Emmie protested that she would be safe. The blacks in the class treated her as a friend. Her companion disagreed. She said she had already been to the black church and the members were celebrating the fall of the Confederacy.

Emmie, startled at this news, finally agreed to return home. She crossed the street with her friend. As the two young women approached the Crump house, Emmie saw Peter, the family's trusted black servant who had worked for her father as long as she could remember. Judge Crump had given the silver-haired slave freedom several years ago. Peter was carrying luggage. Emmie ran up to the black man. Where was he going? What was in the bags?

"These bags are full of silver and Judge Crump's papers," he whispered. "I'm taking them to your aunt's for safekeeping."

Emmie wanted to help, but Peter insisted she go home where she found her mother and brothers stuffing family heirlooms in other bags. Mrs. Crump scolded Emmie for not being home to help. She sent her daughter to aid the others in putting gold coins inside strips of leather that Peter had cut. When he returned, her mother said, she and the other children were to put on the belts and go to their aunt's, accompanied by the manservant.[10]

6

Mayor Joseph Mayo stood at the end of the long table in a corner room upstairs in the Capitol building. He chewed nervously on a chunk of tobacco, then spit a dark stream into the spittoon on the wood floor. He ran his hand across the bald spot on his head and pulled at the stiff collar that rubbed against his throat.

His agitation made his words nearly incoherent as he tried to tell the city council members about the president's cabinet meeting. The president had curtly ordered him to see General Ewell, but he had been unable to locate the general.

David J. Saunders, president of the council, tried to calm the upset mayor, suggesting he take a seat.

"I move the appointment of a committee to wait upon the governor and to request him to retain two regiments for the protection of the city," said Councilman James A. Scott.

His motion was seconded and quickly approved by unanimous vote. Saunders appointed Councilmen Scott, Richard O. Haskins and George K. Crutchfield to form the committee. He also asked the mayor to continue his search for General Ewell.

The committee adjourned and left to consult with the governor, who was in the office on the next floor. The remaining nine men began to talk among themselves. Several lit up cigars. Messrs. Samuel D. Denson and William H. Richardson walked to one of the windows and looked out on the city.

"It's a damnable thing to think we may be looking upon Yankee soldiers tomorrow," Denson said.[11]

7

Private Milton Scruggs was about to hand a slab of bacon to a woman standing below the commissary loading dock. She and her two children waited passively with arms outstretched. Suddenly a boy bolted across the dock and snatched the bacon from the soldier's hands. Scruggs fell back and the youth jumped from the dock and ran through the crowd. The private cursed and swore loudly to his sergeant that they should turn the commissary over to the crowd. The sergeant told him to pull himself together; the army would be gone soon.

The crowd was nearly a hundred strong. Screams and curses pierced the chorus of voices shouting for food. Two women fought over a bag of flour. They fell to the ground, wrestling to pull the bag from each other's arms. It burst and covered them with the ghostly colored powder. Two other women tried to roll a barrel of dried apples through the crowd. It got away from them and rolled into a wall, the top spinning loose, spilling the contents on the street. Children ran up and grabbed the apples, stuffing them in their shirts.

8

The council committee of Scott, Haskins and Crutchfield reported back, accompanied by the governor. The latter had barely taken his seat before the men inundated him with questions. How were the citizens going to protect themselves from looting, from Yankees and from army deserters? Why was the city being abandoned? He attempted to respond but the barrage of angry questions prevented him from answering.

Councilman Nathaniel B. Hill petitioned the governor to authorize two army regiments to remain in the city. He consented to take the request to General Ewell but could not guarantee success. A resolution from the council might help his case.

"Then I so move," motioned Hill.

The motion was quickly carried. The governor attempted to depart, but Saunders said council members had more questions. When the governor pointed out his need to prepare immediately for departure with President Davis, Hill slammed his fist on the table and accused him of abandoning the city. The governor's face became flushed with anger. He was the governor of the state, not mayor of the city, he argued. He was *not* abandoning the city. He was carrying out his duty to be with the president.

The governor gripped the side of the table and his knuckles

went white. There was a hush as he stood, turned and walked briskly out the door, brushing past the mayor.

The flustered mayor complained loudly that he had been to the Customs building, to the War Department, and to General Ewell's house, but he could not find the general.

"Mr. President, I have a motion."

"Yes, Mr. Stokes."*

"Be it resolved that in the event of the evacuation of the city, the council and a committee of citizens appointed by the council president, together with the mayor, shall be authorized to make such arrangements for the surrender of the city as may best protect the interests of the citizens."

There was a brief hush as the word "surrender" was absorbed by the members. It was Councilman Hill who broke the lull.

"I object!" he shouted. "The motion is premature. Is Mr. Stokes giving up already?"

"No, Mr. Hill. I just want to be prepared for the inevitable."

Councilman Richard F. Walker moved that the motion be tabled, but Councilman Scott seconded Stokes's original motion, saying it was sensible. Once the troops left, he argued, the mobs would swarm over the city. The Yankees would be needed to protect the citizens. The majority of the council members voted for Stokes's motion. Saunders appointed William H. Macfarland, Loftin N. Ellett and Judges W. H. Lyons, W. H. Halyburton, and John A. Meredith and the mayor to form the surrender committee.[12]

9

Phoebe Pember walked across Chimborazo Hill between the hospital ward buildings. Several patients passed her, heading towards the city below. She stopped a man hobbling on crutches.

"Young man! Where do you think you're going? You're in no condition to be out of bed."

"The commissary. They're giving away food."

"The commissary is a mile away, down a long hill. Even if you make it down there, you can't possibly walk back up the hill on crutches."

---

*Allen Y. Stokes

"I'm gonna try."

"We have food here. There's no reason to take such a chance. You could fall and hurt yourself further."

"You don't understand, lady. If we don't get the food, the Yankees will. No damn Yankee is going to take what is ours."

Ignoring her protests, the soldier pushed her out of his way and hobbled across the hospital grounds. The matron sighed and continued on her way. Many of the beds filled yesterday were empty; only those patients severely injured or ill remained. The empty beds were in disarray, blankets hanging from the mattresses as a result of hurried exits by the patients.

"My mind had been very unsettled as to my course of action in view of the impending crash," she would write in her diary. "but my duty prompted me to remain with my sick, on the ground that no general ever deserts his troops."[13]

Mrs. Pember struggled with another worry. When the government pulled out that evening, so too would the cabinet official at whose home she was staying. The house would no longer be available to her.

After making her rounds, she took a break and walked about a mile west from the hospital. Along Broad Street she passed block after block of brick row houses, each with a one-story front porch standing only a few feet from the street. At Twenty-Fifth Street she turned south to Grace Street. She walked past the country-like St. John's Church where Patrick Henry had given his famous Liberty speech nearly one-hundred years before. She turned west on Grace Street and stopped at the hill crest at Twenty-Second Street looking down over the city. Later, in her diaries, she noted these observations:

> *Delicate women tottered under the weight of hams, bags of coffee, flour and sugar. Invalided officers carried away articles of unaccustomed luxury for sick wives and children at home. Every vehicle was in requisition, commanding fabulous remuneration, and gold or silver the only currency accepted. The immense concourse of government employees, speculators, gamblers, strangers, pleasure and profit lovers of all kinds that had been attached to the great center, the Capital, were "packing," while those who determined to stay and wait the chances of war, tried to look calmly on, and draw courage from their faith in the justness of their cause.*[14]

10

A few blocks from where Mrs. Pember stood, another woman was watching the chaos from her Church Hill mansion. Elizabeth Van Lew stood on the back porch of her home. Though she wore a full-length black dress, it was not in mourning for the events under way in Richmond. She was smiling.

Miss Van Lew was Southern-born, but Northern-educated. She had no use for the Southerners' cause. When her father died, she freed the family slaves. When the war began, she vowed to do her utmost to help the Union government. That the dark-haired woman was a spy was the consensus among the city's residents. She was suspected of helping Union officers escape after they dug a tunnel under Libby Prison on Cary Street. People called her "Crazy Bet," a nickname she used to her advantage by mumbling to herself so she would be left alone.

She was snubbed by Richmond society and due to questions of her loyalty, she and her mother lived under the shadow of constant threats. She noted them in her diary.

If you spoke in your parlour or chamber to your next of heart you whispered, you looked under the couches and beds. The threats, the scowls, the frowns of an infuriated community—who can write them? I have had brave men shake their fingers in my face and say terrible things. We had threats of being driven away, threats of fire, and threats of death. "You dare to show sympathy for any of these prisoners," said a gentleman, shaking his finger in my face. "I would shoot them as I would blackbirds— and there is something [a]foot up against you now." One day I could speak for my country, the next day I was threatened with death. Surely madness was upon the people! . . .

I was afraid even to pass the prison; I have had occasion to stop near it* and I dared not look up at the windows. I have turned to speak to a friend and found a detective at my elbow. Strange faces could sometimes be seen peeping around the columns and pillars of the back portico.

Once I went to Jefferson Davis himself to see if we could not obtain some protection. He was in a Cabinet session,

---

*Libby Prison.

but I saw . . . his private secretary; he told me I had better apply to the Mayor. . . .[15]

11

In the old city warehouse, the remaining Union enlisted men being held prisoner there waited for their freedom. Word had spread that the Confederate Army was abandoning the city. Vermin were everywhere, in the prisoners' clothing and in their food. A joke in this and other Southern prisons was that the vermin were so plentiful they held regimental drills in the mornings. The men were also tormented by lice and bedbugs, which "crawled over the ground from body to body," their attacks becoming more aggravated as the men became more emaciated. By daylight the vermin could be found and killed. It gave the prisoners something to do. But at night the men had no choice but to suffer their constant attacks.

"We hunted them three times a day but could not get the best of them. They were very prolific and great-grandchildren would be born in twenty-four hours after they struck us," wrote one Union soldier.[16]

12

Traffic jammed every street in the city. Baggage wagons, carts, drays, ambulances—all available vehicles—were put into service to move government papers and money to the Danville Depot. All ages and all classes of people rushed through the streets dodging the vehicles. Citizens who stayed quietly in their homes found their money worthless when they tried to hire slaves and servants to go for food. Others ventured out to stand in long lines at the banks. Those who had gold and silver in their safe-deposit boxes were fortunate. Those who received Confederate dollars and state certificates might as well have thrown them on the piles of papers burning in the street.

Bonfires burned in Capitol Square, fed continuously by box upon box of government papers. The flames rose several stories and the ashes floated over the city and fell like a shower of black snow.[17]

3

As dusk was approaching, I took a break from my work and wandered outside where I encountered James Lyons, a friend of the Davises, and a staunch secessionist.

"Do you plan to stay?" I asked Lyons.

"Most of my friends have advised me to leave, but I feel I must stay here with my family."

"Won't you be arrested by the Yankees?"

"Perhaps. I don't know, but I feel I can better serve my people remaining if I stay."

We walked down to Main Street, discussing further what the next few days could hold for us.

—JOHN BEAUCHAMP JONES.[1]

STREAMS of hissing steam spurted between the iron wheels and bellows of black smoke curled from the stacks of the engines standing at Danville Depot. Soldiers worked rapidly to load government supplies on the boxcars in the railroad yard on the north bank of the James River below the city. As soon as one boxcar was filled, the soldiers moved to another.

Navy Captain William H. Parker, commander of the training ship, *CSS Patrick Henry*, a converted man-of-war, arrived before dusk. He immediately began inspecting the loading process. Walking from car to car he pulled the locked doors to make sure they were secure. When a sailor saluted him, Parker grabbed the navy guard's outstretched hand and swung himself up into the boxcar. Inside were strongboxes. He already knew their contents—silver and gold bullion worth nearly half a million dollars. For 30 weary days the treasury had been under his protection and he was glad to see it intact. Also on board were thousands of dollars in gold belonging to Richmond banks.

"When do we leave?"

"As soon as they complete the train, sir."

"Good. Keep up your guard. I'll be at the president's train or nearby until then."

"Aye, aye, sir."

Parker saluted and jumped from the boxcar. As he walked back along the train, he was shocked at the confused and unsupervised loading operation. There were five other trains besides his own. Most consisted of boxcars or flatcars filled with government employees and soldiers. Many of the cars had arrived only days before filled with supplies for Lee's army—artillery, harnesses, blankets, shoes, clothing and commissary supplies. Now the supplies were lying in unorganized piles between the trains.

Captain Parker approached the yardmaster, Peter Mayo.

"What is to become of these blankets?"

"They will remain here; there is no room on the trains."

"My men have no blankets. Can they take some of these?"

"I have no authority to release them to you, captain."

"Who does?"

"The secretary of war."

"Where can I find him?"

"He's at the train . . . waiting for the president."

The two men walked across the tracks, hopping over rails. They climbed up onto the first passenger car of the president's train; Mayo knocked on the door, and asked to see John C. Breckinridge. The yardmaster relayed Parker's request to the secretary of war.

"Take what you need, captain. And Mr. Mayo . . . if any of the other troops can use any of the supplies, issue them out," Breckinridge said.

"What about the artillery, Mr. Secretary?" Mayo asked.

"I suppose the Yankees will get it."[2]

2

Council President Saunders and the mayor impatiently paced back and forth in the outer room of General Ewell's office in the War Department. Two nails remained in the wall where pictures of General Lee and President Davis had hung. The Confederate flag had also been removed.

"If the orders to fire the warehouses are carried out, the whole city could burn," stammered the mayor.

Saunders recalled the city council's efforts three years ago to persuade the Confederate officials to destroy the tobacco some other way than by burning it.

"The secretary expressed himself willing that the tobacco should be destroyed by putting it in the water if it could be destroyed in that mode," reported Councilman N. B. Hill, chairman of the council committee exploring with the Confederate government means of destroying the tobacco.

Hill's report to the council continued that "at our second interview the committee further represented to the Secretary of War that in the present conditions of the City, crowded as it is with people, including sick soldiers in hospitals and private houses, that there was great danger that in burning the tobacco in the warehouses . . . , many of these sick people might be destroyed. The Secretary did not participate in the fears of the committee."[3]

That the Confederate officials had failed to heed the council's concerns was now painfully clear as Saunders and Mayo sought one last time to plead their case.

The agitation Mayo displayed at the afternoon council meeting had intensified. "What idiot would issue such an order?" he asked to no one in particular, but just as General Ewell entered the room.

"General! You can't do this!"

"My orders are to burn the cotton and tobacco to keep them from the enemy, and I can assure you my orders will be carried out," Ewell shot back.

The general reached down to scratch his leg. The leg was not there, but the itching sensation still came. He had lost the leg in battle at Second Manassas. The wooden replacement was still a cause of consternation.

Saunders pleaded with Ewell to rescind the order. The fires could spread beyond the warehouses, he argued. The general stared grimly at the council president. The orders had come from General Lee's headquarters and they would be carried out, he said. Ewell then left the room. Outside the building an aide helped the general to mount his horse and strapped him securely to the saddle. In his pocket Ewell carried a telegram from General Lee.

It will be necessary for us to abandon our position if possible tonight. Will you be able to do so?[4]

Ewell was now headed to the Danville Depot.

3

Toward the end of the day, Miss Van Lew watched as some young Confederate soldiers in her neighborhood told their families and friends goodbye.

> *I went to the front door of a neighbor—on the steps a woman was sitting in speechless acquiescence. We spoke of the news. She knew only the evacuation of the city.*
>
> *"The war will end now," I said. "The young men's lives will be saved."*
>
> *"I have a son in the army about Petersburg," she replied.*
>
> *I sympathized with her and assured her she might hope for his life, that there would be an end of the terrible words, "the last man must die," which were often spoken and acted upon.*
>
> *She replied, "It would be better, anything would be better than to fall under the U.S. Government." It was useless to talk with her.*[5]

4

It was dusk when President Davis reached the depot by the wide street slanting toward the bridge over the river and away from the city. Most of his cabinet officers were waiting at the president's train. Ill, Trenholm had come in an ambulance but his spirits were good. Benjamin was his jaunty self, smiling through his black beard. Red-faced Mallory was there. Attorney-General George Davis was his usual poised self, and John Reagan chewed while he whittled a stick.

Secretary of War Breckinridge was not going with them. He was mounted on a large, fat horse. The secretary was speaking with the president, both trying to obtain some news of Lee's army before the train left.

Farewell parties and curiosity seekers milled around the train. The president climbed into the creaky passenger car and seated himself on one of the benches. He began to pen a letter to Varina.

My Dearest wife:
I sent a message to Mr. Grant* that I have neglected to
return the cow and wished him send for her immediately.
Called off on horseback to the depot; I left the servants to
go down with the boxes and they left Tippy—Watson came
willingly. Spencer against his will. Robert, Alf, V.B. &
Ives got drunk. . . .

He also wrote two other letters, one to Mrs. O'Melia
instructing her to "pack and store as your discretion may
indicate" the furniture in the executive mansion, and the other
to Mayor Mayo commending Mrs. O'Melia "to his kind care."[6]

Captain Parker walked up to Breckinridge to advise him of
the train's immediate departure.

"All the trains are packed, sir. I don't think there is empty
space anywhere. Soldiers and clerks are everywhere, on the
top of the boxcars and even the engines. I believe some are
even hanging on by their eyelids," the captain said.[7]

5

Admiral Semmes's sailors crawled around on their ships like
worker ants, gathering up supplies. The men were leaving
homesteads which they had inhabited for months, and in cases
for several years. Ahead was the unfamiliar—marching for
miles on land. Hammocks were lashed and blankets compactly
rolled. Haversacks and canteens had to be improvised. Bread,
meat and any other food they could find was stuffed in pockets
and blankets. Rifles were issued each sailor.[8]

6

A young rider turned his mount at Ninth Street and galloped
up Franklin Street. Darkness engulfed the buildings as rider
and horse wove through the wandering throngs of remaining
people. He brought the horse to a halt in front of the three-story
brick house. Candles shone behind the drawn curtains in the
right front room. A gaslight dimly lit the building.

The rider dismounted, brushed off his uniform and took a

---

*James Grant lived across the street from the Davis mansion and lent the
family one of his milk cows.

pouch from his saddlebags. He climbed the stairs of the front porch and pulled on the bell. A woman opened the door slightly and peered out.

"Percy Hawes! Come in!"

Percy followed General Lee's daughter, Mildred, into the parlor where a white-haired woman smiled from her rocker. A knit shawl hung around her shoulders and a lace cap covered her head.

"I have a letter from the general," Percy said, handing it to Mrs. Lee.

The courier and Mildred looked on as the general's wife read the letter.

"Your father says there's no hope of saving Richmond, and he agrees with you that we should leave," Mrs. Lee said.

"I have to tell you, Mrs. Lee, I agree with the general."

"I know you mean well, Percy, but I'm an old woman with arthritis. It would kill me to leave this house now. Besides, where would I go?"

"There must be many safe houses, friends who would welcome you."

Mrs. Lee smiled at Percy and patted his hand.

"Enough of this talk, Percy. You must be hungry. Have some tea with us. Mildred, go get this young man something to eat."[9]

7

Leyburn and a friend walked along the outskirts of the depot, looking for a train to board.

"Can't we get in here?" asked Leyburn at a boxcar of a quartermaster train.

"No! Impossible! We're crushed to suffocation."

They walked to another boxcar.

"Won't you just let one gentleman in here? His home and family are up in the country, and he is anxious to get to them," pleaded Leyburn.

"No! No! We're too full already. This car is marked for 14,500 pounds, and we have too many now. We'll break down before we travel five miles," argued a clerk at the car door.

Leyburn and his friend trudged on in despair. A few yards along, however, Leyburn stopped. Coming towards them was a man with a lantern escorting two gentlemen.

"Be alert!" whispered Leyburn. "When he pushes them up, I'll push you up immediately behind them, as if you are with them."

As the trio passed, Leyburn and his friend got into step behind them.

"Hey! You up there," shouted the man with the lantern. "Let these gentlemen in. They must go with the president's party."

Grumbling, the clerk reached down and grabbed the hand of the first and pulled him into the boxcar and then the other. Leyburn pushed his friend up into the car.

"You're not one of these men. Get off!" shouted the clerk.

"I am in now and in I will stay," Leyburn's friend said. He pulled back his coat to expose a pistol tucked in his belt. The clerk argued no more.[10]

8

The Crump family had gathered in the parlor of their Broad Street home for their nightly Bible reading. Peter, the family's freed servant, sat on a chair in the corner, his head bowed. Other servants stood near the door. The children sat cross-legged on the floor around their mother. Emmie was opposite in a chair, the Bible on her lap. She continued reading from Psalms 17:

> *My ravenous enemies beset me. They shut up their cruel hearts, their mouths speak proudly.*
>
> *Their steps even now surround me; crouching to the ground, they fix their gaze, like lions hungry for prey, like young lions lurking in hiding.*
>
> *Rise, O Lord, confront them and cast them down; rescue me by your sword from the wicked; by your hand, O Lord, from mortal men . . .*

9

A man and a woman staggered along East Main Street dragging a burlap bag filled with items they had plundered from several stores. They looked as if they had walked out of the pages of a novel by Charles Dickens. Their clothes were ragged and dirty, their hair stringy and unkempt. A scar zigzagged across the man's cheek; several teeth were missing. The woman's face and body were puffy and her tangled hair spilled in disarray down her back. The stench of perspiration and unwashed bodies hung around them.

The man tilted his head back and took a drink from a brown glass bottle. He held up the bottle and peered into it. He handed it to the woman and she, too, tilted the bottle and searched inside.

The woman threw the bottle and it crashed against the stone wall of the Customs House where it shattered and fell in splinters.

"I could use some of them jewels, Pa."

Her husband bowed and pointed towards Mitchell and Tyler's Jewelers store. The building was dark, the front window smashed. The man cleared the remaining glass splinters by swinging the burlap bag around the edge of the window. He then helped the woman onto the windowsill; put his hands on her rump; squeezed playfully and shoved her through the window.

As the couple searched the jewelry store, other small groups plundered other stores along the street. At a tailor shop in the next block, suits were thrown out of the door and grabbed by waiting arms. Two muscular country women grabbed the sleeves of the same coat and began a tug of war. The bigger woman won and went tumbling down on the street. She rolled over laughing and nearly knocked over two passing scavengers.

Across the street four men hammered at the door of another jewelry store.

"On three," one of them said.

"One, two, three."

Two of the men shoved against the door with their shoulders. The door shuddered, but did not give.

"One more time."

Again the two men ran at the door. It burst open and they stumbled to the floor. The remaining two men joined them inside just as a blast of light came from the back of the store. It was followed by a cracking sound and splinters of wood flying from the door frame. A second and a third shot quickly followed. The intruders screamed and began crawling as fast as they could for the door, slithering on their bellies like four lizards. Another shot took out the transom window.

"Next time I'll shoot to kill," the store owner yelled.

10

Lt. Colonel John Cheeves Haskell, returning from visiting a friend at Drewry's Bluff, came riding up Main Street with a few of his men. When he came upon the rioting and looting, he ordered his men to charge their horses along the buildings to drive the looters away. Women screamed and ran into the street, but many cursed the soldiers, and when the horsemen passed, they resumed their ransacking.

Haskell turned his horse at the end of the block and started to order another charge, but he feared harm to his men. The crowd was too large and too mean. The cavalrymen continued up the street. As they approached Mitchell and Tyler's, the colonel noticed a woman backing out of the window. He drew his saber and galloped his horse, catching the woman across the rear with the flat side of his sword. She stumbled and her plunder spilled to the street. Curse words rang in Haskell's ears as he rode on.[11]

11

"Mr. President, it's time to go," Breckinridge said, saluting a farewell.

The president nodded.

He climbed on the creaky car. The signalman swung a lantern from side to side, and the engineer waved his left hand in acknowledgment. With his right he pushed the throttle. The engine belched a cloud of gray and black smoke; it lurched forward and the giant iron wheels spewed sparks as they ground the rails to catch hold. One after another, the couplers between the cars clanged.

The engine lurched again and the wheels caught hold. Slowly the train inched forward, straining under the weight of hundreds of thousands of pounds. Yard by yard the train moved away from the depot until the engine switched tracks to a bridge across the James River. The engineer pulled a rope and the steam screamed from the whistle.

Secretary of War Breckinridge slapped the back of his horse and it trotted through the railroad yard. As the horse reached the canal basin at Ninth Street, the secretary slapped the horse again and it galloped down the towpath heading west along the river, the soft lights of the city fading fast.

Another horseman was preparing to take the same route. Governor Smith mounted his horse at the Capitol and rode down Shockoe Hill towards the canal. He planned to take the towpath to Lynchburg and to catch up with the presidential party in Danville. He was greatly concerned about leaving his wife at the Governor's mansion, but she had told him, "I may feel as a woman, but I can act like a man. Attend to your public affairs and I will arrange our family matters."[12]

12

Lieutenant John S. Wise, 18-year-old son of ex-Governor Henry A. Wise, watched as President Davis's train passed through Chesterfield County. Through the train windows he could see the Confederate leader.

> *Mr. Davis sat at a car window. The crowd at the [Bon Air] station cheered. He smiled and acknowledged their compliment, but his expression showed physical and mental exhaustion. . . .*[13]

13

Southern correspondent Thomas Cooper DeLeon had traveled through the Confederacy for four years reporting on the war, and now the writer was witnessing the fall of Richmond as he had the fall of Atlanta.

> *Who . . . will ever forget that bitter night. Husbands hastily arranged what plans they might, for the safety of family they were forced to leave behind; women crept out into the midnight, to conceal the little jewelry, money or silver left them, fearing general sack of the city and treachery of even the most trusted negroes. For some knew but that a brutal and drunken mob might be let loose upon the hated, long-coveted Capital, in their power at last . . . !*
>
> *So men went forth into the black midnight, to what fate they dreamed not, leaving those loved beyond self to what fate they dared not dream!*
>
> *But even in that supreme hour—true to her nature and true to her past—the woman of Richmond thought of her*

hero-soldier; not of herself. The last crust in the house was thrust into his reluctant hand; the last bottle of rare old wine slyly dropped into his haversack. Every man in gray was a brother-in-heart to every woman that night!

. . . I rode by a well-remembered porch, where all that was brightest and gayest of Richmond's youth had passed many happy hours. There was Styles Staple; his joyous face clouded now, his glib tongue mute—with two weeping girls clinging to his hands. Solemnly he bent down; pressed his lips to each pure forehead . . . , threw himself into their mother's arms, as she had been his own as well; then, with a wrench, broke away and hurled himself into the saddle. . . .[14]

14

Dr. Minnigerode held the prayer book in one hand and glanced down at the pages, but he knew the words by heart.

"Do you Walter Taylor take Elizabeth Shelton to be your wife? To have and to hold in sickness and. . . . "

The couple stood before the minister in the parlor of the Lewis D. Crenshaw home at Eleventh and Clay streets. Taylor, a member of General Lee's staff, wore his tailored dress uniform consisting of gray pants and coat. Brass buttons ran down both sides of the coat front, and gold thread signatures curved along the sleeves and the collar. The coat hung about four inches above the knees. Miss Shelton was dressed in a simple, full-length white dress. She looked lovingly up at her husband as Dr. Minnigerode pronounced them man and wife.[15]

15

Seventeen-year-old Lelian M. Cook of Blackstone, Virginia, was visiting the Hoges at their house at Fifth and Main streets. In her diary she noted that few people slept this night after seeing the government and military leaving.

"I laid down at 3 o'clock. Our soldier friends were coming in at all hours to bid us good-bye. I hardly knew the meaning of the word [evacuation] until then," she wrote.[16]

16

In the stillness after midnight, the sounds along the Union
and Confederate lines east of Richmond were those of melodi-
ous strains of brass and string instruments. The serenades
drifted from the trenches of both sides.

The music was a cover.

As the band members played, their compatriots slipped
quietly out of the trenches. Confederate soldiers stole away in
retreat. Union soldiers moved in a wide circle around the
Confederate lines in the direction of Richmond. When the
charade ended, there was only one soldier left in the trenches,
a Union drummer boy who lay curled against a dirt wall,
exhausted in sleep.

1. *St. Paul's Episcopal Church in 1865. Confederate President Jefferson Davis was attending services here when a messenger brought him General Robert E. Lee's telegram stating his lines at Petersburg had fallen.*

2. *This drawing of Richmond in 1865 was printed in Harper's Weekly magazine. It shows the Capitol at right and the City Hall in the center. The view is from the south end of Fourth Street.*

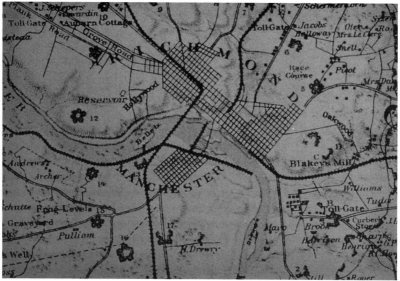

3. A Confederate engineers' map of 1865 shows the city covered a relatively small area when compared to its present-day size. South of Richmond was the town of Manchester.

4. The Confederate Naval Yard stood on the banks of the James River below Chimborazo Hill in the eastern section of Richmond.

5. *Jefferson Davis was a U.S. senator when southern states began to leave the Union. He was inaugurated as Confederate president in February 1861.*

6. *Varina Davis was 10 years younger than her husband. They were married in 1845, 10 years after the death of Davis's first wife, Sarah Knox Taylor.*

Monday, April 3

A MASS of people pour across Mayo's Bridge to escape the Confederate capital. It is a wretched crowd of retreating soldiers, scavengers, looters, escaped prisoners and women and children. Richmond is now a city in turmoil. Many citizens are departing in fear of the Union soldiers and impending occupation. Others are fleeing because they fear for their lives as the collapse of law and order quickens. Others are carrying off their stolen loot.

The mood in the city has changed. Sharing has given way to a take-what-you-can mentality. Respect for personal property has all but vanished. Look at those passing. That hag there. The feathered hat she wears was stolen from a shop on Main Street. The deserter behind her, his arms laden with brass candlesticks. They were probably stolen from a house; maybe, God forbid, from a church.

General Lee is in retreat, moving southwest to Amelia Court House. President Davis's train is steaming toward Danville.

4

THE Confederate soldier swung the sledgehammer and smashed the lock on the one-story-high wooden double doors. The lock fell to the ground and soldiers pushed open the doors of the public warehouse near the canal basin at Ninth Street. As the doors slid back, the smell of tobacco permeated the air. The soldiers fanned out, the light from their torches stabbing at the darkness. The center of the building was open to the roof, drawing air from the doors like the draft of a chimney.

Four soldiers began working quickly to ignite the stacks of tobacco scattered inside the warehouse. The dry leaves caught fire readily when torched. The soldiers continued firing the bales as they backtracked to the doors; the flaming tobacco exploded as the fire sucked oxygen from the air and leapt up the center of the building to the roof.

The Confederates proceeded from the first warehouse to torch Mayo's and Dibrell's warehouses on Cary Street in Shockoe. The darkness surrounding the buildings faded in the brilliant light. The soldiers cheered.

2

"Tallyho!" yelled a man from the second-story window of a building near Shockoe Creek. He teetered, a silk hat cockeyed on his head. Two women looters below looked up just in time to jump from the path of a cartwheeling wooden barrel. The barrel splintered and the liquid splashed over the cobblestones. The first barrel was quickly followed by another and another. A familiar smell permeated the air and one of the women reached down to touch the liquid. She tasted it.

"It's whiskey!" she cried.

Many others dropped to their knees to taste. A woman leaned on her hands and slurped up the liquid flowing down the street. She turned and smiled, droplets falling from the side of her mouth and hair. Her ostrich-feathered hat and lace shawl, stolen that day, were drenched with whiskey.

Men rolled barrels out of the building and knocked in the heads with sledgehammers, freeing more whiskey to feed the growing stream. Each time a case of bottles crashed to the street or a barrel was broken open, the crowd, ever growing larger, cheered.

Three Confederate soldiers staggering up the street in retreat saw the cheering crowd and stopped. Many in the crowd paused and turned to look at the men in uniform. The soldiers began to unsling their rifles and several women in the crowd became frightened. One by one the men undid their knapsacks and took out their cups. Then with a howl, they dropped their rifles and ran up the street to join in the drinking.

3

An ear-piercing explosion erupted in the middle of the James River. Pieces of wood flew through the air and a gaping hole appeared in the deck of the training ship, *Patrick Henry*, anchored near Rocketts Landing. A black mushroom of smoke, joined by yellow and red flames, gushed from the hole and spewed into the dim light of the early morning. A second explosion rumbled across the water and the sound wave shook a small boat rowed by naval cadets who had left the ship moments before. Simultaneously the Confederate ironclads were blown up down river near Drewry's Bluff.

Sallie A. Putnam wrote of the explosions in her diary.

> *The noise . . . was like that of a hundred cannon at one time. The very foundations of the city were shaken. . . . The Patrick Henry, a receiving ship, was scuttled, and all the shipping at the wharves was fired except for the flag-of-truce steamer, "Allison."* [2]

4

The shoulder-to-shoulder line of people crossing south on Mayo's Bridge halted with the explosions. The mob shifted to the east railing to watch.

A horse-drawn ambulance approached the south end of the bridge. The driver, seeking to cross toward Richmond, was blocked by the mob. He snapped his whip again and again to make the horse move.

"Get out of the way! Get out of the way!" the driver shouted at the oncoming people.

A man in the crowd raised his fist at the driver. "You get out of the way. You're going the wrong way. Can't you see we are leaving the city?"

The driver raised his whip and cracked it near the man's ear. "Let me through!"

He snapped the whip again and the horse jumped ahead. The mob parted. The body of a general, dressed in baggy pants and a calico shirt made by his wife, rocked back and forth in the rear of the ambulance as it bounced across the bridge.

5

Nellie Grey was too afraid to sleep. She sat on the window seat, watching out over the city from her room at the Arlington House. The events she was witnessing made her curl up tightly, drawing up her knees to her chin. The munition explosions continued to light up the sky, and these lights were joined by the flames that leapt from the tobacco warehouses. The fires jumped from roof to roof. The Gallego Flour Mill was lit like a candle. Dust from the stored flour flared and blew in a high ball of flame like a Roman candle. The sky was daylight-bright.

6

The fire chief was at his wit's end. All he could do was order his men to move the three pumpers back from the spreading flames.

"Turn the hoses on these buildings," he ordered. "Water them down! Water them down!"

The firemen trained the hoses on the buildings a block from the Gallego Mill. Six firemen, three on each side of the pumper, pushed and pulled, up and down, on the bars to create suction to pull the water through the hoses laid down to the canal. The water shot out of the brass nozzle about 10 feet and then arched down to a slow sputtering dribble onto the street. Laughter rupted from the crowd of drunkards and scavengers gathered to watch.

The fire chief ran over to the pumper and joined his men.

"Push, pull! Push, pull!" he encouraged them.

The water shot from the nozzle again, sputtered, and then flowed in a steady stream to the second floor of the building. The firemen swung the hose back and forth, splattering the building's front with water. The fires were so intense they continued to leap from roof to roof north toward Main Street. The hot air rising from the fire generated its own wind and one wooden building after another exploded in flames. The chief ordered his men to fall back. They struggled to move the pumpers. No one in the crowd offered to help.

The heat singed the firemen's beards and hair. The men pushed the pumpers up the hill. In the hurry to retreat from the fire, no one thought to uncouple the hose from the pumper. It broke loose and swung wildly like a striking snake as water sought escape.

7

Assistant Paymaster G. Powell Hill stood with his cousin, Henry, outside the entrance of the Customs building on Main Street. The two men watched as the mobs moved up and down the street. Not one door or window in any business stood unshattered. The street was littered with glass, clothes, paper, broken furniture and liquor bottles. About the only thing missing from the discarded heaps in the street were shoes. A pair now commanded over $3,000 in Confederate currency.

"You see it yet?" asked Powell Hill.

"No."

They heard shouts from down the street, and soon through the smoke could see an ambulance charging towards them. The driver snapped the whip and the horse raced on. There was fear on the driver's face—fear the crowd would stop him and take the horse.

"Whoa! Whoa!" he shouted when he saw the Hills. A cloud of dust rolling behind the ambulance caught up with it and enveloped the vehicle. Coughing and dusting themselves off, the Hills ran to the back of the ambulance and pulled open the door. Inside was the body of Powell Hill's uncle, General A. P.

Hill, mortally wounded in the Battle of Petersburg the day
before.

"Good, God, Henry! Why didn't you tell me he wasn't in a
coffin."[3]

8

A bright light flashed outside Constance Cary's window, and
the concussion from the explosion shocked her from sleep. The
window panes shattered, showering her with glass.

The sky outside lit up again and the house shook. The sound
of more glass breaking filled the house. She leapt from her bed,
ran downstairs and out into the street screaming.[4]

9

"We must find a coffin," shouted Powell Hill over the noise
of the explosions and fires, "and give him a decent burial."

His cousin shook his head in assent as the two men shut the
door to the ambulance. They left the driver to stand guard while
they searched. Shop after shop stood open. The doors to
Belvin's Furniture Store, one of the finest in the city, were ajar.
The contents had been ransacked. The two Hills entered the
store and stumbled around in the darkness.

Near the door they found a stack of wooden coffins the store
owner sold to the war's many widows. They pulled out a
medium-sized pine box and Henry Hill lifted it to his right
shoulder. His cousin led the way out and they carried it through
an alleyway to avoid looters.

When they reached the ambulance, Powell Hill opened the
door and climbed in. His cousin shoved the coffin in beside his
uncle's body and then jumped in the vehicle. The two men
lifted the body, rank and stiff with rigor mortis, and lowered it
into the box and nailed it shut. It was an arduous task.[5]

10

The southeastern wind whipped the flames up Main Street as
building after building caught fire. The looters ran ahead of the
conflagration, scavenging all they could. Front walls peeled off
like old paint and waves of flaming debris crashed into the
street. The air filled with sparks; transported by the wind, these

ignited roofs of houses blocks away. Hundreds of structures were now in flames. Grayish-black smoke rolled over the city choking even those inside their homes with windows closed.

11

"Sir! I think Richmond is burning. The sky is red."

The Union soldier was bending down by the open flap of the tent, speaking to General Edward H. Ripley. The commander of the Ninth Vermont Regiment rose from his desk where he was writing daily reports.

"Richmond on fire, lieutenant?"

"There's a fire in that direction. Look at the sky."

In the distance a faint column of flames shot up. Shortly after, the Union soldiers heard the muffled sound of an explosion. The general knelt down and put his ear to the ground. The earth shook and he looked up.

"Something hellish is going on, lieutenant. See if you can find out what."

The lieutenant heard shouting as he started to run for his horse. He turned to see a buggy approaching rapidly. A black man stood in the buggy, his legs apart to balance himself, holding the reins and urging the horse on.

"They is runnin' from Richmond! They is runnin' from Richmond! Glory. GLORRRY!" shouted the black man.[6]

12

The mayor took a white handkerchief and tied it to a stick. He placed the stick in the lead carriage and climbed aboard. The six men, John A. Meredith, W.H. Halyburton, William H. MacFarland, Loftin Ellett and W. H. Lyons and the mayor, were dressed in the same clothes worn to church services nearly 16 hours earlier. The men climbed into two carriages. The mayor snapped the whip across the back of the old horse. The carriage jerked forward and rolled out of the Capitol grounds towards Broad Street. The second carriage followed. They turned east on Broad and began a rumbling roll down the steep hill towards Shockoe Bottom. Drunks and looters stepped out of the way as the mayor cracked the whip. The old nag could barely keep ahead of the carriage as it gathered speed.

At the bottom of the hill the carriages rumbled across the

wooden planks of the bridge crossing Shockoe Creek. The six men struggled to hold on. Turning on Seventeenth Street, they sped along, reaching Main Street where they charged east below Church Hill.

13

The line of 12,000 Union soldiers moved slowly and quietly along New Market Road in Henrico County east of the city. It had been an eerie night. They had passed seven rows of enemy trenches, but all had been abandoned by the Confederates. Ahead of the Union soldiers was a red glow in the sky that occasionally flared. It was almost too quiet; this was war, yet no one tried to impede their movements.

The men walked in single file, leery of land mines left by the retreating army. Ahead of this main group rode horsemen attached to the Fourth Massachusetts Cavalry. With them was Major Atherton H. Stevens, provost to General Godfrey Weitzel and Major E.A. Graves, aide-de-camp. Every 15 minutes scouts were sent ahead to look for signs of the enemy. None were found, but Major Stevens was still wary.

14

Crowds of evacuees moved shoulder to shoulder with straggling groups of retreating soldiers across Mayo's Bridge. Others traveled west along Cary Street to Henrico and Goochland counties.

Four men, still wearing the gray pants that denoted their occupation, boarded a boat in the Tidewater connection of the canal near Sixteenth Street. They manned poles, pushing the bateaux eastward. The boat slipped quietly along the canal, unseen by those passing across Mayo's Bridge overhead. The bateaux slipped toward and under the bridge, and the men brought it to a halt. Each grabbing a rope, the men climbed to the bank and tied the boat to the bridge pilings. They lit torches and threw them into the craft, where dry piles of debris caught fire quickly. The men stole away into the crowd above.

The fire leapt from the boat and licked at the underside of the bridge. A flame shot up along the bridge railing, startling the crossing throngs. Cries of "fire" filled the air and those approaching the bridge began rushing to cross before it ignited fully. Then the bridge and ground shook violently. The water rippled from the concussion of shells exploding in the arsenal several blocks away. One shell arced through the air and exploded directly over the bridge, sending the pedestrians into panic. Women and children silently grabbed each other, their fright-gripped throats frozen.

15

Very few were sleeping as early morning dawned at Chimborazo Hospital. The waves of explosions and concussions even broke into the sound sleep of patients sedated for pain. Phoebe Pember spent the dark hours visiting the wards, comforting those unsettled by the invading noises. Perhaps it was the memory of Fisher that made her stay. It was two years ago. His leg had been badly mangled by a shell explosion. He was spared amputation, one of the lucky ones. Ten months later he was walking, despite the doctors' assurances to the contrary.

"He had remained through all his trials, stout, fresh and hearty, interesting in appearance and so gentlemannered and uncomplaining that we all loved him," Matron Pember recalled.

But then one night Mrs. Pember was called to his bedside. She found him lying there uncomplaining, a jet of blood spurting from his leg. The walk that afternoon in the ward had unsettled a jagged piece of bone and it had cut through an artery. Immediately she put her finger to the wound to shut off the bleeding. When the surgeon came, he said the artery was too deeply encased in flesh to be repaired. Shaking his head, he said in a whisper that the boy would die.

Mrs. Pember told Fisher the truth.

"How long can I live?" he asked.

"Only as long as I keep my finger upon this artery."

For a long pause he was silent. Finally he spoke.

"You can let go."

But Mrs. Pember couldn't, "not if my own life had trembled in the balance."

Her eyes filled with tears. She became numb and cold from staying in the same position, holding her finger on the artery.

"Finally the pang of obeying him was spared me and for the first time during the trials that surrounded me for four years, I fainted away," Mrs. Pember later wrote.

"Ma'am! What's happening now? Have the Yankees come?" asked a wounded Confederate soldier. His question returned her thoughts to the present.

"No, soldier. But if they do, you won't be hurt."

"I wish I was home. I miss my family. . . . I'm scared I won't ever see them again."

"We're all a little scared," Mrs. Pember assured him. "It's the fear of the unknown. Try to go to sleep."

"You know, ma'am," began the soldier again, "I pray each night we will defeat the Yankees, and though I can't bear the Yankees, I believe some of them are Christians and pray as hard as we do. I don't know what to think of our prayers clashing."[7]

Mrs. Pember smiled at the philosophical statement.

"I believe God hears all prayers. We do not know why He chooses to answer some and not others. We can only trust in His infinite wisdom."

"Will you pray with me, ma'am?"

"What prayer will we say?"

"The 'Our Father'."

Mrs. Pember sat in a chair beside the soldier's bed. She took his hand in hers and the two began praying. Others in the ward joined them.

16

Major Stevens raised his right hand in a signal for the cavalrymen to halt. A scout galloped up New Market Road toward them.

"Carriages coming, sir. They're six men and there's a white flag tied to each vehicle."

The Union soldiers watched the darkened road where New Market Road and the Osborne Turnpike connected. Soon they could make out the silhouette of the lead carriage. Two cavalrymen ventured out to meet the carriages.

"Halt! Identify yourselves!"

The carriages slowed and stopped in front of the two soldiers. The old horse in front of the lead carriage panted from pulling the vehicle up the long hill from Fulton Bottom.

"I am the mayor of Richmond and we've come to see the Union commander."

"Follow me."

The carriages were driven a hundred yards farther up the road.

"Are you the Union commander?" asked Mayo upon seeing Stevens.

"I am Major Stevens, an aide to General Weitzel."

"These gentlemen and I represent the citizens of Richmond. We are here to ask your help," explained the mayor.

The mayor held up a piece of wallpaper. On the unflowered side, Stevens read this message:

To the General commanding the United States Army in front of Richmond:
 General:
 The Army of the Confederate Government having abandoned the City of Richmond, I respectfully request that you take possession of it with an organized force, to preserve order and protect women and children and property.

> *Richmond, April 3, 1865*
> *Respectfully,*
> *Joseph Mayo, Mayor.*[8]

17

The Union drummer boy turned over and lay flat on his back. As a bird whistled softly overhead, the youth stirred. His eyes flicked open and he stared up at the trees and the pinkish, pre-dawn sky. He sat up abruptly, looking to his left and to his right. He was alone in the trench.

The boy jumped up and grabbed his drum. He ducked his head under the strap attached to the drum and climbed out of the trench. He ran through the woods towards Richmond, the drum bouncing off his leg.

18

For two hours Rebecca Jane Allen had sat anxiously at the window. A nearby building was ablaze and the fire was spreading. Now, she could watch no longer. The boys were asleep in the back room, each to a bed. They had gone to sleep directly after supper, having eaten one potato apiece. Rebecca Jane's little money bought less and less each day. Her husband was somewhere on the other side of the river, retreating with General Lee's troops. It had been two months since he had written last, sending her $9, most of his monthly pay of $11.

"Mama?"

"Come on. Get up!" she said as she softly smacked the soles of the boys' feet.

They grumbled, but rolled out of bed.

"Mama, I'm hungry," cried John, the oldest.

"I know, but we haven't got time to eat now. We have to leave the house."

She dressed the youngest boys quickly, then herded them all toward the front of the house.

"We're going on a little trip," she said.

"Why? I want to go back to sleep. It's still dark," protested William.

Rebecca Jane lifted Bobbie in her arms and took William by the hand.

"Open the door, John."

He turned the door knob and pushed the door open.

"Mother! Fire!"

"I know. That's why we have to leave."

"Is our house going to burn?"

"I hope not, but we can't take any chances."

Holding Bobbie in her arms and pulling William along beside her, Rebecca Jane hurried the boys across the street. In an empty field in sight of the house, she sat them down on a stack of wood.

"John, hold onto Bobbie. I'll be back."

Mrs. Allen ran back to the house. She gathered up clothes and a few pieces of stale bread. Four times she repeated the trek, each time adding to the heap of possessions beside the boys. On her fifth trip she stopped to let two carriages pass on Main Street. Hastening toward the center of the city, each carriage carried three persons. On each vehicle, a white flag fluttered in the wind.

After crossing the street for the last time, Mrs. Allen sat down on the woodpile. The boys gathered around her and began to nibble on the bread.[9]

19

With Governor Smith holding tight, the horse sped along the towpath through western Henrico County. Driven by fear to put distance between himself and Richmond, Smith stared ahead, searching the darkness. The unseen river crashed over nearby rocks. Apprehension caused his mind to play tricks. Trees became Yankee soldiers. Limbs were arms reaching to grab him. The roar of the water over Bosher's Dam was a cavalry of horses charging toward him.

Smith smacked the back of the horse. The governor's face was flushed, his underarms moist. The roar of the water charging over the 10-foot-high dam was now on his left. The Kanawha Canal's Nine Mile Locks were on his right. Above the locks the river sent a current of water into the canal, and the towpath ended there.

He slapped the horse harder. The animal charged into the air over the canal. It hit the water short of the far bank and the water's surface split. The horse came to a slow-motion stop, but the governor's body hurled on. Smith tumbled through the air, a scream tearing from his throat. He hit the top of the grassy, far bank and rolled into the woods. Wet and muddy, bruised and angry, he lay gasping for breath. His heart pounded at 150 beats a minute.

The horse climbed the bank and limped over to its rider. Water streaming from the animal showered the governor. A few minutes later Smith was on the horse again. His fright dissipated and Smith laughed loudly in relief of being alive.[10]

7. *Phoebe Yates Pember met opposition from the male-dominated medical staff, but proved herself to be a strong leader as a matron of Chimborazo Hospital.*

8. *Chimborazo Hospital was one of the largest military hospitals during the war, treating more than 77,000 patients.*

9. *A woman volunteer reads a letter from home to a wounded Confederate. Women played a major part in the care of the sick and wounded at Chimborazo and the other half-dozen city hospitals and homes.*

10. *Dr. Charles Minnigerode was leading the service at St. Paul's Church when word came to evacuate the city.*

11. *Mayor Joseph Carrington Mayo wrote the official surrender message on the back of a piece of wallpaper.*

12. *Dr. Moses D. Hoge's service at Second Presbyterian Church was interrupted by the news that Petersburg had fallen.*

13. *Governor William Smith fled the city on a horse.*

14. *General Richard S. Ewell ordered warehouses fired.*

15. *Admiral Raphael Semmes ordered the naval ships blown up.*

16. *Mrs. Robert E. Lee. She refused to leave Richmond.*

17. *Seeing Union soldiers entering Richmond, Elizabeth Van Lew, "Grant's spy in Richmond," had her manservant hoist the Union flag at her Church Hill mansion.*

18. *General A.P. Hill was killed in Petersburg April 2. His body was brought to Richmond during the raging fires and given a temporary burial in Chesterfield County.*

5

DAWN exploded over Richmond. The city shook to its foundations as a blast more powerful than any ever heard in the capital tore through the powder magazine below the Alms House on Shockoe Hill. Thousands of pounds of powder ignited in a blinding flash. The magazine walls and roof exploded. Stone, mortar and slate scattered like shrapnel. A black pillar of smoke mushroomed and obscured the rising sun.

The noise of the explosion deafened the screams of the men who had ignited the powder. Their bodies went flying into the valley below along with the boulder behind which they had sought protection. The concussion shattered their skulls and their bones. In all, a dozen persons died.

Circles of pressure spread out from the magazine as the explosive force reverberated through the air, bending trees and shattering every window on the east and south sides of the Alms House at the northern end of Fifth Street. Blocks away on Broad Street, house walls cracked and plaster fell from the ceilings.

Emmie Crump bolted upright in her bed, startled, unsure as to whether she was awake or having a nightmare. The house continued to shake as if in the aftershocks of an earthquake. She could hear shouts from other family members, but couldn't bring herself to answer. It should be light outside, she thought, but there was only darkness.

Emmie looked around the room. Her eyes followed a new crack in the ceiling until it stopped just overhead. A foot-sized piece of plaster was missing. She scanned down toward the bed. Pieces of plaster lay on the bedside table. One larger piece lay on the floor, along with a pewter cup in which she always placed her favorite brooch. She leaned down and gently swept away the plaster. The brooch was underneath. She picked it up and gently rubbed the white powder away, examining it closely. Except for a tiny scratch, the brooch given to her by her grandmother was unscathed.

Emmie swung her feet to the floor and stood up, losing her balance as another explosion rocked the house. She ran out of the room and downstairs, where the rest of the family had gathered. Beverley was at the front window watching as a large black cloud blotted out the light from the rising sun.

Mrs. Crump told them that Peter said the powder house had exploded and they should stay in the house.[1]

2

Joseph Anderson stood behind a line of his workers at the Tredegar Iron Works below Gamble's Hill. A strikingly handsome man of 34, he was officially a Confederate general. Midway through the war he was ordered back to Richmond to run the vital iron works. The foundry produced cannons and iron plates for ships as well as other arms for the Confederacy. Tredegar, one of the South's few rolling mills, was the most important one.

Anderson and his men, even some of the slaves, were armed. Throughout the night they had stood guard against arsonists and looters. Now massive fires were advancing upriver. From their foundry they could see buildings burning along Main and Cary streets and the canal. The early morning sun was obscured by the rolls of smoke.

One of the workers pointed toward the Richmond-Petersburg railway bridge that crossed at a point two blocks downriver from the foundry. Smoke was rising from the north end of the covered wooden bridge. The smoke turned to flames as the dry wood ignited. Laughing, the worker observed that the Union army would have a hard time moving up from the south with all the bridges burning.

"That's what worries me," said Anderson. "We're going to need their help to stop this holocaust."

Anderson moved among his men directing them to set up bucket brigades to quench any fire started by sparks.[2]

3

A large mob had gathered at the corner of Fourteenth and Cary streets near Mayo's Bridge. The bridge was not their destination, however; they were after food and the commissary building was their target. A woman yelled for the men to tear down the doors. Three Confederate deserters rushed the doors. They were padlocked. The men pushed and pulled on the doors, but the lock held fast. Others joined, rocking the doors back and forth. Finally there was a loud crack as one of the boards gave way. The crowd cheered, and the group at the doors labored even harder. Then the doors gave way and the men and women crowded inside.

A brigade was formed and hams, bacon, whiskey, flour, sugar and coffee were passed out. Fights broke out as one person tried to grab from another. The fights spilled into Fourteenth Street.

Captain Clement Sulivane and a small band of rear guard briefly watched the looters from across the street until the sound of wagon wheels drew their attention toward Main Street. The soldiers took up positions, fearing the approach of the Yankee Army. The wagons turned south onto Fourteenth Street.

"They're ours!" a soldier shouted.

"General Gary's coming! Hold your fire!" Captain Sulivane ordered.

General Martin W. Gary's command consisted of several hundred troops who had held the defenses east of the city. The South Carolinian had been ordered to retreat once the government and other Confederate troops left the city. The first of his brigade consisted of ambulance wagons sent forward in preparation of his final rush for the bridge. As the wagons turned on Fourteenth Street, Captain Sulivane jumped on his horse and ordered several of his soldiers to follow. They charged toward the mob, yelling for the people to clear the way.

The ambulance wagons were followed by Gary's cavalry with the general in the lead. As he passed Sulivane, the general touched his hat and called out.

"All over, goodbye; blow her to hell."

Sulivane and his men began walking across Mayo's Bridge toward the island in the middle of the river. Along the way they set fire to combustible material set at strategic sections of the bridge.[3]

4

Phoebe Pember walked along the eastern edge of Chimborazo Hill, seeking a brief respite from her hospital duties. The hill provided a view eastward of a commanding sight. Just below was Fulton Bottom with block after block of two- and three-story, Federal-period homes. Some were built more than a century before, after William Byrd II of Westover established Richmond at the head of the James River falls.

To the southeast at Rocketts Landing and across the river at the navy yard, a few ships of the Confederate Navy were still burning. Mrs. Pember let her eyes follow the road that paralleled the James River and cut through Fulton Bottom until it became New Market Road and rose steeply up the opposite hill. It was the "road of plantations," leading to Westover, Shirley and Berkeley plantations and Williamsburg.

The hospital matron turned to walk back to the wards, but stopped after a few steps. Again she stared at the crest of the opposite hill and squinted her eyes in an effort to sharpen her vision. There a tiny but unmistakable figure stood. A man on a horse. Then another and another. Then one holding a flag.

"The Union army," she thought, taking off in a run back to the hospital.[4]

The small group of Union cavalrymen stood halted at Almond Creek on New Market Road, just east of Rocketts Landing. The advance group of 40 were clothed in relatively new uniforms. These healthy-looking men, astride their fresh horses, stood in striking contrast to the ragged, hungry Confederate soldiers leaving the city.

A rider approached from their rear, rode past the two columns and halted alongside Major Stevens.

"Sir! I have advised General Weitzel of the message brought from the Richmond mayor. The general is not far behind, and he wants you to proceed to the city."

"Thank you, Mr. Prescott."* Stevens stood in his stirrups and turned toward his men. "We have orders to enter Richmond. Keep a tight formation and a good watch."

Stevens had a difficult time not giving a yell and charging toward the city. They had been fighting for many weary months to take Richmond and end the war. His men would be the first to enter the Confederate capital.[5]

---

*Lt. Royal B. Prescott

6

The black man opened the door of the smokehouse behind a home at the corner of Nicholson and Main streets in Fulton. In one hand the servant carried a slab of bacon.

He froze when he heard the sounds, dropping the bacon. He stared ahead in disbelief. Approaching the intersection were two columns of horsemen. Their uniforms were not the familiar gray he was accustomed to seeing. They were blue! The gray-haired man ran up to the approaching cavalrymen and reached out his hand. A soldier reached down and touched the slave's head. Tears streamed from the black man's face as he walked alongside the soldiers.

The burning city drew the cavalry like a magnet as they passed below Chimborazo Hill. A mile behind this advance group, a line of soldiers crossed the hill overlooking Fulton Bottom. They popped up over the hill, one after another, like dandelions springing up in a field. Within minutes the hill was covered with hundreds of infantrymen. At the lead was General Godfrey Weitzel.[6]

7

The fire in the twenty-first block of Main Street had spread. The Allens watched, cowering in the field, but turned away from the fire as the sound of approaching horses became audible.

Rebecca Jane watched, partly out of curiosity, partly out of the fear she hid from her children.

"Soldiers coming, Ma?"

"I think so, John."

"Ours?"

"Yankees, I think."

"Yankees?"

"Yes. See, their uniforms are blue."

Mrs. Allen pulled her youngest to her bosom to comfort him. The cavalry passed, leaving the Allens in their refuge.

8

Black reporter Thomas Morris Chester watched as Weitzel's troops marched down Osburn Turnpike.

Along the road on which the troops marched, or rather double timed, batches of negroes were gathered together testifying by unmistakable signs their delight at our coming. Rebel soldiers who had hid themselves when their army moved came out of the bushes, and gave themselves up as disgusted with the service. The haste of the rebels was evident in guns, camp equipage, telegraph wires, and other army property which they did not have time to burn.[7]

9

General Weitzel's regiment came to a halt at Gillies Creek east of Richmond. A scout approached.

"Sentry ahead."

A young soldier stepped out from behind a tree a hundred yards up the road. He wore a thin, tattered Confederate uniform. A rifle was cradled in his arms. As he looked around and saw the approaching Union soldiers, he stood transfixed. The scout and another soldier approached him cautiously. The sentry did not raise his rifle or make any threatening moves.

"Are you an officer?" the Confederate asked.

"No, but General Weitzel is just behind us."

"Why have I not been relieved?" the sentry asked.

"What?"

General Weitzel rode up. "Give me your rifle and go home," the general said. "The war is over for you."

"Over?"

"Over. Your army has left the city."

The Confederate looked at his rifle. He seemed confused. One of the Union soldiers walked slowly over to him and gently lifted the rifle from his arms.

"Go home, soldier," General Weitzel said.

The Confederate walked over to a tree stump and sat down. He placed his head in his hands and stared at the ground as the Union soldiers rode on.[8]

10

Admiral Semmes stood on the deck of the small steamer as it and two others moved upriver, carrying the last of his men. As the boats approached Mayo's Bridge, they cut to the south bank. The sailors had one of the few vantage points from which to see an unobscured rising sun. Its light was reflected in the southeast-facing windows of the homes on Gamble's Hill and the reflections mimicked the fires below the hill. The Capitol was hidden by smoke, along with most of the city.

The boats reached the bank and Semmes and his sailors disembarked. Several sailors threw lighted torches into the boats and pushed them out into the current. The boats drifted downriver in flames.

Hundreds of men and women who sought refuge in Manchester, across the river from Richmond, stood watching the sailors gathering on the shore. A current of horsemen from the retreating army filed slowly by, watching the sailors. They began to make jokes about the "old salts" and whether their sea legs could carry them over land.

Semmes ignored the taunts, but he knew his men looked ridiculous to these land soldiers. The sailors were laden with pots, pans, mess kettles, bags of bread, chunks of salted pork and various other items. Some carried such a load that they staggered.

The admiral ordered his captains to get the men in formation. As he inspected them, he wondered how far they could march. He told the sailors that the army had left them no means of transportation. Anyone who fell behind in the march would be on his own.

As the sailors began moving out, one of their comrades came running back from scouting the rail yard. He had found an engine, he yelled. He ran back toward the yard with the others close behind.

The men stopped quickly after rounding a shed. There stood a small rusting yard engine. Semmes walked around the engine inspecting it closely. He climbed into the cab and tested the throttle.

"Any of you ever run a railroad engine?" he shouted to his men.

"Couldn't be much different than running the boiler on a ship," answered a seamen.

Semmes ordered the other sailors to go through the rail yard to search for boxcars. They found four, chasing out several deserters and citizens who had taken refuge. There were pleas for the sailors to take them along.

Semmes' navy now had a train of one engine and four dilapidated boxcars. Wood was stripped from nearby fences, thrown into the engine's boiler and fired. The sailor engineer pulled the whistle rope, pushed the throttle forward and let out a Rebel yell. The train strained for about 200 hundred yards down the track, and then the engine began to lose power. A cloud of steam spewed from one side of the boiler.

"Get off, admiral! She's goin' to blow!"

Semmes and the engineer jumped from the still-moving train. The engine hissed and sputtered as it slowed to a stop, but the boiler did not explode.

"Anyway to repair it?" asked Semmes.

"I don't see no way, sir. We don't have nothing to patch it with."

"Well, start looking again. We found one engine, maybe we'll find another."

They did. Several sailors discovered a new engine hidden inside a shack behind a stack of wood. The sailors ran down the tracks and uncoupled the four boxcars from the damaged engine.

Shortly after eight o'clock, the "navy" train pulled out of the Manchester Station, heading west along the James River. About two miles from the city the rails cut southwest toward Danville.[9]

11

Naval Cadet Hubbard Taylor Minor, Jr., had been left behind when the other cadets departed. Suffering from dysentery for two weeks, he had been sent to a hospital. Sick as he was, he was determined to leave Richmond and catch up with his shipmates.

> *. . . I determined to go down to the Danville depot by 6:30 on Monday Morning so I went to work & put up 2 white under shirts 1 flannil overshirt & . . . a Jacket & pr. of Pants with a Towell & my shawl & a Blanket this being all I could possibly carry in my weak state[.]*
>
> *. . . When I got to the depot I was told that the last train had left[.] . . . I went over to Manchester & found there several trains & got a board of one of them[.] last night nearly every store in Richmond was broken into & robbed & this morning many large buildings were on fire[.]*[10]

12

Clerk Jones walked along Broad Street, feeling alone and lost. All around were people, many of them blacks who were celebrating. A few lone whites were selling food and clothing. Four men, dressed in suits, proffered goods from their carpet-bags. The prices were too steep for those remaining in the city, most of whom now had only worthless Confederate money.

"Want to buy a sack of 'tatoes, mister?"

Jones stopped to examine the woman's goods. The hag was wearing a tattered brown dress. Her hair was tangled and dirty, but topped with a bonnet full of chicken feathers.

"Where did you get these?" Jones asked.

"From the man at the commissary. He gave 'em to me."

"What else you got?"

"Dried apples and flour."

The two haggled briefly before agreeing on a price. Jones fished out the money and handed it to the woman. She grinned at him, showing several missing teeth.[11]

13

Mrs. Robert C. Stanard sat beside the front window of her home at Eighth and Franklin streets. She watched the swirling fire and smoke outside with the same coolness that had made her one of the war's most admired hostesses.

Even on this morning of devastation, she wore a satin dress. One might have thought she was waiting for guests to arrive for afternoon tea or an evening of music. Her social gatherings had been approved by the Confederate government as a diversion for officers on leave or recuperating from injuries.

During these last months when citizens waited daily in lines for food, Mrs. Stanard had held "muffin matches" and "waffle worries," parties that brought together the military and civilians to share whatever food they had.

The era of evening parties had slipped away as the Union Army moved ever closer to the city, but Mrs. Stanard never seemed to fret. She smiled as she now sat recalling gatherings where some of the prettiest belles of Richmond had flirted and danced with some of the most handsome Confederate officers.

Mrs. Stanard took the handsome, bearded DeLeon by the arm as he entered the foyer, and walked with him to the parlor.

"Mr. DeLeon. Where have you been—Charleston? New Orleans?"

"Here for the past two weeks," he answered.

"What? And you have just come to see me? Shame on you! I believe you have been avoiding me for fear one of these young ladies might snatch you from bachelorhood."

"Mrs. Stanard, I still cannot get accustomed to this Southern phenomenon of the unmarried element composing the majority of the guests. It seems to me the young people have seized the society while the elders' heads were turned and have run away with it," chuckled DeLeon.

"Since I can remember, Mr. DeLeon, only unmarried people have been allowed to party. The married folks do the requisite amount of visiting and teaing-out; and sometimes even rise in our wrath and come out to dinner. But I must say, I enjoy these young people. They keep me young."

Three local amateur musicians played in one corner of the drawing room, giving a credible rendition of the latest Southern songs, along with an occasional "Dixie," to which the guests stood and cheered.

A lively young woman, her bosom pushed up and partially exposed, as was the fashion, walked over to DeLeon and Mrs. Stanard.

"Mr. DeLeon! Oh, Mr. DeLeon! I heard tell you were here, and I said to myself, 'I must ask Mr. DeLeon to tell us about Charleston'."

"Yes, you must," added the hostess.

DeLeon sat his teacup on the mantle and began a discourse of his latest travels through the Southern cities. The musicians stopped playing and the guests gathered around to hear.[12]

"Mrs. Stanard!" The servant woman called nervously from the parlor door. "The fire, Mrs. Stanard. Shouldn't we leave?"

The sound of the servant's voice called her back to the present. She looked out the window.

"Don't worry so, Mary. There's still time."

"But I'm so frightened of the noise and fire."

"Alright, Mary. You come upstairs with me and we'll pack."

Decisively, but in no hurry, Mrs. Stanard led the way up the steps from which she had often announced engagements, births and other lively news.

Once in her bedroom she pulled a trunk from under her canopy bed and told the servant to place her dresses carefully therein. The black woman hurried to fill the trunk, glancing towards the windows frequently as she worked.

"Carefully, Mary. Carefully fold the dresses. There's time."

"But Mrs. Stanard if we don't hurry, we're surely gonna burn up with the house."

Mrs. Stanard sorted through her jewelry, placing the valuable pieces in handkerchiefs that she tied and laid among the dresses. The two women carried the trunk downstairs and outside the house. Once on the sidewalk, Mrs. Stanard sat down on the trunk, pulled up her gloves and adjusted her hat. She watched the burning city through her lorgnette. It was only after the United Presbyterian Church across the street burst into flames and its steeple crashed to the ground that she allowed Mary to flag down a wagon driver to take them away.[13]

14

Around eight in the morning the Hill cousins arrived at the home of Powell Hill's father on the James River near the Bellona Arsenal in Chesterfield County. They left the ambulance wagon parked on the road leading to the house and went in to find the elder Mr. Hill at breakfast.

"You two look wretched," Powell's father said.

"General Hill has been killed. We have his body. We sent you a message."

"I didn't get it."

"The general was killed at Petersburg yesterday."

"And you haven't buried him?"

"There was no time. It took hours for the ambulance wagon to get to Richmond. We were able to get a coffin only then."

The elder Hill told them to bury the body in the yard. A proper burial in Hollywood Cemetery could be held later. The two cousins went outside where a manservant dug a grave. The coffin was lowered into the shallow hole as the senior Hill joined them. Each of the Hills picked up a handful of dirt and threw it on the coffin, and the manservant then took the shovel to finish filling the hole.[14]

6

*F*ROM high above Main Street Miss Van Lew saw Weitzel's troops. She yelled for her manservant and the young black man came running out onto the portico. He found Miss Van Lew pointing to the street below. Upon spotting the soldiers he let out a cheer.

"The flag! Go get the flag!" Miss Van Lew shouted.

The manservant ran back into the house and down to the basement. He rapidly raked back scraps of wood with his hands and uncovered a trunk. Throwing open the top, he dug through rags to a burlap bag in the bottom. The manservant lifted the bag out and looked inside, his eyes moistening as he saw the flag of stars and stripes. Tucking the bag under his arm, he ran back upstairs, vaulting up the three flights two steps at a time. Leaning far out of the third-story window, he attached the red and white cloth to some rope and raised the flag to the top of a pole on the roof.

Miss Van Lew looked up as the wind caught the flag and straightened it out. Unaware of the flag, the soldiers rode toward the Capitol.[1] Some of the neighbors, upon sighting the offensive Union symbol, gathered around the Van Lew house, trampling through the garden. Their demeanor was nasty. Miss Van Lew stepped forward to confront them.

"I know *you*, and *you*," she said, calling out their names. "General Grant will be in town in an hour. You do one thing to my home, and all of yours will be burned before noon!" The neighbors, apparently convinced, went home.[2]

2

Ahead of Major Stevens's cavalry was a wall of flame and smoke. East Main Street from halfway through the 1500 block west to the 800 block was burning. Most the building fronts lay crumbled and fires from both sides of the street fed smoke and flames into the inferno. It was a hellish scene.

Stevens turned to another officer, Lieutenant Livingston De Peyster of the Thirteenth New York Artillery.

75

"You have the flag?"

"Yes, sir!" said De Peyster as he slapped his saddlebag.

The cavalry moved off in a gallop, scattering the crowd in the street, and turned north on Fifteenth to avoid the flames. Still the fire was so hot it singed the hair on some of the riders, who persisted without pause as they made their way to the bottom of Capitol Hill. Major Stevens led the charge up the hill to the prize. The cavalrymen wove their horses through groups of citizens who had gathered on the hill in refuge. The area looked like an encampment of lost souls.

De Peyster and Captain Loomis L. Langdon halted their horses at the south entrance of the building. De Peyster unbuckled his saddlebag and took out the large folded flag. The two men dismounted and ran through the entrance. History pulled them through the first floor hall. Adrenalin pumped them up the winding marble staircase to the roof. The trapdoor was already unlatched.

The two officers crawled across the slanted tin roof; the wind rippled the plumes of Langdon's cap. Langdon held the rope tightly as De Peyster hooked on the flag. As it rose, the flag unfurled in the wind. It contained 31 stars sewn in the shape of a star and was the same flag that had been flown over New Orleans when the Union Army took that city on April 27, 1862.[3]

3

The Crump children stood in their backyard watching over the fence. A cavalryman dashed by on Twelfth Street and turned at the corner towards the Capitol grounds. The children stood on their tiptoes to see better. Emmie's brother, Beverley, tapped her on the shoulder and pointed towards the Capitol building.

"Up there," he said.

Emmie looked up at the roof and saw the two Union soldiers raising the flag. She started to yell, but no sound came out of her mouth.

"MOTHER!" she finally screamed.

Mrs. Crump ran out onto the back porch to witness the children yelling and pointing to the soldiers.

"Get in the house," Mrs. Crump said.

The children protested at first, but then filed reluctantly past her into the kitchen.

"Lock all the doors and shutters," she ordered.

Emmie and Beverley ran around the first floor turning locks and closing shutters. As Emmie walked away from the front door, there was a pounding.

"Should I answer it?" she called out.

"It could be a Yankee," cautioned her cousin, Kate.

There were further thumps in rapid succession.

"Let me in! Let me in!" a female voice cried.

Emmie turned the door handle and as it released the catch, the door was flung open, and a young woman burst into the house. Maggie Cary, only a few years older than Emmie, ran into the hall. She threw her arms around Mrs. Crump and began sobbing.

"The Yankees have taken the Capitol. They are everywhere."

Maggie stepped back and pushed the curls away from her face.

"Please, Mrs. Crump. Can I stay here?"

"I thought you were staying with the governor and Mrs. Smith."

"The governor has gone."

"You left Mrs. Smith alone?"

"She'll be alright. I can't go back. The Negroes are in a frenzy, and the soldiers are everywhere. Can't I stay here?"

Mrs Crump decided she couldn't send Maggie back out into the streets, at least not now.[4]

4

Tears streamed down Nellie Grey's face as she watched the Union flag being raised over the Capitol.

> *. . . We knew what that meant! The song, "On to Richmond!," was ended—Richmond was in the hands of the Federals. We covered our faces and cried aloud. All through the house was the sound of sobbing. It was as the house of mourning, the house of death. . . .*
> *The saddest moment of my life was when I saw that Southern cross dragged down and the Stars and Stripes run up above the Capitol. . . . As I tell this my heart turns sick with the supreme anguish of the moment when I saw*

*it torn down from the height where valor had kept it waving
for so long and at such cost.*

Was it for this I thought that Jackson had fallen?; for
this that my brave, laughing General Stuart* was dead—
dead and lying in his grave at Hollywood under the very
shadow of that flag floating from the Capitol, in hearing of
these bands playing triumphant airs as they marched
through the streets of Richmond, in hearing of those
shouts of victory? O my chevalier! I had to thank God that
the kindly sod hid you from all those sights and sounds so
bitter to me then. I looked toward Hollywood with streaming eyes and thanked God for your sake. Was it to this end
that we had fought and starved and gone naked and cold?
to this end that the wives and children of many a dear and
gallant friend were husbandless and fatherless? to this end
that our homes were in ruins, our state devastated? to this
end that Lee and his footsore veterans were seeking the
covert of the mountains?[5]*

Also watching the Union march into Richmond was another
woman who preferred not to be identified. Her memoirs were
later recorded by Richmond *Examiner* editor Edward A. Pollard, who gave her the fictitious name, "Nathalie."

*Stretching from the Exchange Hotel† to the slopes of
Church Hill, down the hill, through the valley, up the
ascent to the hotel, was the array, with its unbroken line of
blue, fringed by bright bayonets. Strains of martial music,
flushed countenances, waving swords, betokened the vic-
torious army. As the line turned at the Exchange Hotel
into the upper street, the movement was the signal for a
wild burst of cheers from each regiment. Shouts from a
few negroes were the only responses. Through throngs of
sullen spectators; along the line of fire; in the midst of the
horrors of a conflagration, increased by the explosion of
shells left by the retreating army; through curtains of
smoke; through the vast aerial auditorium convulsed with*

---

*General Stonewall Jackson was wounded during the Battle of Chancel-
lorsville, and died May 10, 1863. General J.E.B. Stuart, wounded at Yellow
Tavern May 11, 1864, died the next day and was buried in Richmond's
Hollywood Cemetery.

†The Exchange Hotel was at Fourteenth and Franklin streets.

*the commotion of frightful sounds, moved the garish
procession of the grand army, with brave music, and
bright banners and wild cheers. A regiment of negro
cavalry swept by the hotel. As they turned the street they
drew their sabres and with savage shouts, and the blood
mounted even in my woman's heart with quick throbs of
defiance.*[6]

Walking along with the lead unit, the 368th Colored Troops,
under Lieutenant Colonel B. F. Pratt, was reporter Chester.

*There were many persons in the better-class houses who
were peeping out the windows, and whose movements
indicated that they would need watching in the future.
There was no mistaking the curl of their lips and the flash
of their eyes.*
*. . . The soldiers cheered lustily, which were mingled with
every kind of expression of delight. The citizens stood gaping in wonder at the splendidly-equipped army marching
along under the graceful folds of the old flag. Some waved
their hats and women their hands in token of gladness. The
pious old negroes, male and female, indulged in such expressions: "You've come at last"; "God Bless you"; "I've
not seen that old flag for four years"; "It does my eyes
good"; "Have you come to stay?";"Thank God," and
similar expressions of exultation*[7].

As the Union troops reached the burning section of the city,
the impact of the conflagration became evident, and Chester
observed it.

*The flames, in spreading, soon communicated to poor
and rich homes alike. All classes were soon rushing, into
the streets with their goods, to save them. They hardly laid
them down before they were picked up by those who
openly were plundering everyplace where anything of
value was to be obtained. It was retributive justice upon
the aiders and abettors of treason to see their property
fired by the rebel chiefs and plundered by the people whom
they meant to forever enslave. . . .*
*The leader of this system of public plunder was a colored
man who carried upon his shoulder an iron crow-bar, and
as a mark of distinguishment had a red piece of goods
around his waist which reached down to his knees. The*

mob, for it could not properly be called anything else, followed him as their leader; moved on when he advanced, and rushed into every passage which was made by the leader with his crow-bar. Goods of every description were seized under these circumstances and personally appropriated by the supporters of an equal distribution of property. Cotton goods in abundance, tobacco in untold quantities, shoes, rebel military clothing and goods and furniture generally were carried away by the people as long as any thing of value was to be obtained.[8]

7

General Weitzel arrived at City Hall on Broad Street shortly after the flag was raised over the Capitol building. The handsome, bearded man walked up the steps to meet the mayor. Mayo escorted the general to his office. Weitzel sat down at the desk and thanked the mayor, but waved him out of the office. The general began dictating a series of memoranda to his aide.

General Ulysses S. Grant:
We took Richmond at a quarter past eight this morning. . . .[9]

8

Judith W. McGuire periodically drew up enough courage to venture outside of the boardinghouse. She later recorded in her diary what she had witnessed.

Union men began to show themselves; treason walked abroad. . . . The Colonel and B. had just gone. Shall we ever meet again? Many ladies were now upon the streets. The lower part of the city was burning. . . . the pavements were covered with broken glass; women, both white and coloured, were walking in multitudes. . . . with bags of flour, meal, coffee, sugar, rolls of cotton cloth, etc.; coloured men were rolling wheelbarrows filled in the same way. I went . . . towards the depot; and as I proceeded shouts and screams became louder. The rabble rushed by me in one stream. At last I exclaimed, "Who are those shouting? What is the matter?" I seemed to be answered by a hundred voices, "The Yankees have come."[10]

9

A woman referred to as "Matoaca," walked to the damaged War Department building at Ninth and Franklin streets to retrieve some letters.

The desk was open . . . the papers were found and I started homeward. We saw rolls of smoke ahead, and trod carefully the fiery streets. Suddenly my companion caught my arm, crying: 'Is not that the sound of the cavalry?' We hurried, almost running. Soon after we entered the house, some one exclaimed:

"God help us! The United States flag is flying over our Capitol!"

I laid down my head on Uncle Randolph's knee and shivered. He placed his hand lightly on my head and said: "Trust in God, my child . . . ." He had fought for that flag in Mexico. He stood by Virginia, but he had always been a Unionist . . .[11]

10

Lelian Cook saw her first Union soldier between eight and nine o'clock.

. . . Federals came dashing up to this corner on splendid horses and turned down Fifth Street. After that, others came through on horseback, and some on foot, but all very quietly. There was no yelling, as we expected.

Just before a squad passed here on foot, someone had thrown "our flag" on the pavement. Several of the Federals took it up, but threw it down again. I don't know what became of it at last. I felt as if I would have given anything to have gone and picked it up.[12]

11

The Union officer rode his thoroughbred horse down Broad Street Hill towards Shockoe Bottom. Eight other soldiers rode along with him. They drew stares from whites and exultant greetings from blacks. He gave a courtesy salute, but no smile. He looked disgustedly at the blacks and whites alike carrying off stolen goods, at the drunks staggering in the street, at the litter, at a broken wagon, its dead horse covered with flies. The smell rankled his nose, and his eyes itched from the soot and smoke.

The soldiers rode across the bridge over Shockoe Creek and on up the street to Church Hill. They turned on Twenty-third Street and rode to Grace Street. They stopped about mid-block in front of a large mansion.

The officer dismounted and walked up the curved staircase to the front door. He rapped on the door and then straightened his uniform. Out of the corner of his eye he noticed movement in one of the windows, but by the time he looked the curtain was closed. The door was opened slowly by a young black girl.

The officer introduced himself and said he was looking for Miss Van Lew. She had gone to town, the girl said, to the Confederate War Department. The officer told several of the Union soldiers to post guard around the house and took the others with him back to the city to look for Miss Van Lew.

7

LINE after line of Union soldiers paraded along lower Main Street as federal troops continued to pour into the city. The military instrumentalists played "Yankee Doodle," "John Brown's Body" and other rousing songs. With each song there were cheers from the blacks standing three and four deep along the street. Others, now freed men and women, hung out of the windows of two- and three-story buildings. A company of black soldiers came into view and the crowd broke into a frenzy of yelling and dancing. Many ran into the street to shake hands with the passing soldiers and to slap them on the back. Women kissed and hugged them.

A few whites who had come out of curiosity to watch, stood silently, cowering in the background. The white women wore black, many with veils covering their faces. The white men grumbled under their breath and cursed the blacks and Union soldiers.

2

On the rooftops of houses on Third and Fourth streets, residents of Gamble's Hill tried to save their homes by pouring water on blankets spread across the shingles. A black servant emptied his bucket. The owner handed him another bucket of water and took the empty one. The servant dumped the water on the blanket. A flaming ash landed on the blanket's edge, sizzled and died out.

3

General Weitzel sat back in the wooden chair behind the mayor's desk. A Confederate flag still stood in the corner, the mayor's oversight.

"Read the orders back to me."

Maj. Gen. Godfrey Weitzel, commanding detachment of the Army of the James, announces the occupation of the

83

City of Richmond by the Armies of the United States, under the command of Lieut.-Gen. Grant. The people of Richmond are assured that we come to restore to them the blessings of peace, prosperity, and freedom, under the flag of the Union.

The citizens of Richmond are requested to remain, for the present quietly within their houses and to avoid all public assemblages or meetings in the public streets. An efficient provost guard will immediately re-establish order and tranquility within the city.

Martial law is, for the present, proclaimed.

Brigadier General George F. Shepley, United States Volunteers, is hearby appointed military governor of Richmond.

Lieut. Col. Fred P. Manning, Provost Marshal General, Army of the James, will act as Provost Marshal of Richmond. Commanders of detachments doing guard duty in the city will report to him for instructions.

By command of
Major General Weitzel.
D.D. Wheeler, Assistant Adjutant General.[1]

Weitzel added several more orders, including one directing troops to help fight the fires.

The general, Wheeler and Major Stevens left the office and walked down the hallway; an elderly civilian clerk approached from the opposite end. The clerk saw the officers and moved to the side, cowering against the wall. He looked down at the wooden floor as they passed.

"Good morning, sir," said General Wheeler. The man did not answer.

As the officers crossed Broad Street, sounds of "Yankee Doodle" greeted them from the distance. Parading up Franklin Street at that time was the First Vermont Brigade of the Twenty-Fourth Corps, led by Brigadier General Edward H. Ripley. As on Main Street, Franklin Street was lined with blacks dancing and singing.

The three officers arrived at the Capitol grounds just as the Twenty-Fourth entered the square. The officers walked into the building through the north entrance amid salutes from soldiers gathered around stacked rifles. The sound of the hard heels of the officers' boots hitting the marble floors echoed off the walls.

Midway through the building they climbed the stairs to the next floor. There they crossed to the south double wooden doors; walked through and stood on the edge of the south portico.

Below them were several hundred encamped citizens and an equal number of soldiers. A cheer rose from the soldiers when the officers came into view; the whites stared curiously.

"General! Hold that pose!" yelled a photographer who had traveled with the Union soldiers into the city.

The photographer ducked under the black cloth of his large wooden camera atop a wooden tripod. He adjusted the lens at the end of the bellows while looking through the 8 × 10 groundglass, which showed an upside down view of the scene. The photographer's head came back into view as he reached into a case, taking out a glass negative holder and inserting it into the back of the bulky camera. He held up his left hand to keep the attention of the officers and squeezed the rubber bulb; the shutter clicked.

The photograph froze the historic moment. It showed five Union soldiers standing on the portico. Below them in the picture were 10 other soldiers, one leaning casually on a temporary wooden fence.[2]

"Thank you, general."

The photographer moved his contraption down the hill. Setting it up again, he took another photograph. When the glass plate was developed, it showed 13 Union cavalry horses tied to an iron fence at the bottom of the Capitol grounds. Behind the animals were the brick shells of buildings, some obscured by smoke. Four trees along the street were burned of their spring leaves.

4

One after another, the foundry workers turned over the water buckets and sat on them to rest. Joseph Anderson walked from man to man, worker and slave, thanking them for protecting the iron works. They had fought and quenched the fires. Except for several small shacks, the workers had prevented the fires from destroying anything of substantial value.

Anderson wiped soot from his face and ran his hand through his hair. He started to speak, but his words were drowned out by a loud explosion. He and several workers were knocked to the ground by the concussion. Another projectile whistled overhead and exploded near the river's edge. The men ran for cover. There was another explosion and another.

Barely a block from the foundry, munitions and gun powder in the arsenal at Seventh and Canal streets had ignited in a holocaust.[3]

5

Examiner editor Edward A. Pollard watched the fires from near Capitol Square.

> *Long lines of negro cavalry swept by the Exchange Hotel, brandishing their swords and uttering savage shouts. These shouts, the roar of devouring flames, the endless procession of plunderers passing from street to street, tugging away the prizes they had drawn from the hellish circle of the fire, made up an indescribable horror. Here were the garish Yankee troops sweeping up towards the Capitol Square, with music and wild cheers; everywhere, almost, the pandemonium of fire and pillage; and in the midst of all the wild agony, the fugitive distress of women and children rushing towards the open square for a breath of pure air, all that was now left them in heaven's great hollowness. And even that was not to be obtained there. The air, even in the square of the Capitol, was almost choking; and one traversed it blinded by cinders and struggling for breath. Beneath the trees, on the sward, were piles of furniture, dragged from the ruins of burning houses; and on carpets, stretched on the slopes of the hill, were family groups, making all sorts of uncouth arrangements to protect their little ones, and to patch up, with broken tables and bureaus, some sort of home in the open air.*[4]

Fellow journalist, Arthur Henry of the New York *Tribune*, sat at a window in the Spottswood Hotel at Eighth and Main streets. Only a change in the wind had spared the hotel from the fire. The location gave Henry a good view of the chaos. He completed and reviewed a dispatch for his newspaper before sending it off through the telegraph office.

> *Our army was greeted with enthusiastic cheers by the populace. The colored population were exceedingly jubi-*

lant and danced for very joy. . . . That part of the city along the river front known as the main business part was one vast sheet of flames.

What with the roaring and dashing and clashing, burning and tumbling buildings, the shoutes of our soldiers moving up the main street to the Capitol, the music of Union bands . . . , the shoutes of welcome and excitement of the people was a scene of grandeur and magnificence never to be effaced from our memory. . . .[5]

DeLeon made these observations:

A dense pall of smoke hovered low over the entire city; and through it shone huge eddies of flames and sparks, carrying great blazing planks and rafters whirling over the shriveling buildings. Little by little these drew closer together . . . , and livid flame roared and screamed before the wind . . . , licking its red tongue around all in its reach and drawing the hope—the very life of thousands into its relentless maw!

Should the wind shift, that rapidly-gaining fire would sweep uptown and devour the whole city; but, while the few men left looked on in dismayed apathy, deliverance came from the enemy. The regiments in Capitol Square stacked arms; were formed into firesquads; and sped at once to points of danger. Down the deserted streets these marched; now hidden by eddying smoke—again showing like silhouettes, against the vivid glare behind them. Once at their points of work, the men went at it with a will; and—so strong was force of discipline—with no single attempt to plunder reported! . . .

Whatever the citizens may vaguely have expected from Grant's army, what they received from it that day was aid—protection—safety! Demoralized and distracted by sorrow and imminent danger; with almost every male absent . . . the great bulk of Richmond's population might have been homeless . . . , but for the disciplined promptitude of the Union troops.[6]

Within the business district, hundreds of structures were damaged or destroyed. These included the Bank of Richmond, Traders' Bank, the Bank of the Commonwealth, the Bank of Virginia, Farmers' Bank, the American Hotel, the Columbian

Hotel, the *Enquirer* newspaper building, the *Dispatch* office and job rooms and the *Examiner* office, the Confederate Post Office building and the State Courthouse on the edge of the Capitol grounds.[7]

6

The old man and his black servant stood in front of Pratt's Castle on Gamble's Hill. They were surrounded by furniture—a dining room table and four chairs, a chest of silverware, a dressing table, a carved oak mirror—and two gentleman's suits. They were tired and wet; their hair was singed and their faces smudged with soot. Neighbors spoke comforting words. Two Union soldiers stood guard over their possessions.

The black servant hung his head. His arms and shoulders ached. His forehead hurt from a burn. Every now and then the two men looked back towards the remnants of their home, four walls, smoke curling from the smoldering embers inside.

A covered wagon came up the street and the driver stopped the Union vehicle in front of the small gathering. He and two sentries began loading the furniture.

"Where will you go?" asked a neighbor.

"My sister's in Goochland. We'll go to the farm and start over."

7

The Union officer looking for Miss Van Lew approached Capitol Square with his men. One of them pointed toward the smoldering War Department building, and there they found a woman in a black dress picking through documents.

"Miss Van Lew?"

The woman stood up and looked at the officer.

"Yes?"

"General Grant sent me to see to your safety."

It was noon.

8

*T*HE Union soldier tacked the first of the notices to a tree at Eighth and Grace streets. The papers were signed by Brigadier General George F. Shepley, newly appointed military governor of the city. The first order dealt with efforts to quell fires and invited any citizen "interested in preservation of their beautiful city" to join in the effort.

The soldier read through the other orders:

II. No person will leave the city of Richmond, without a pass from the office of the provost-marshal.

III. Any citizen, soldier, or any person whatever, who shall hereafter plunder, destroy, or remove any public or private property of any description whatever, will be arrested and summarily punished.

IV. The soldiers of the command will abstain from any offensive or insulting words or gestures towards the citizens.

V. No treasonable or offensive expressions insulting to the flag, the cause, or the armies of the Union, will hereafter be allowed.

VI. For an exposition of their rights, duties and privileges, the citizens of Richmond are respectfully referred to the proclamation of the President of the United States in relation to the existing rebellion.

VII. All persons having in their possession, or under their control, any property whatever of the so-called Confederate States, or any officer thereof, or the records or archives of any public officer whatever, will immediately report the same to Colonel Manning, provost-marshall.

In conclusion, the citizens of Richmond are assured that, with the restoration of the flag of the Union, they may expect the restoration of that peace, prosperity, and happiness which they enjoyed under the Union of which that flag is the glorious symbol.[1]

2

Squads of Union soldiers marched throughout the city posting guards at key intersections, government buildings and the

89

homes of citizens who requested protection. A squad of black soldiers, commanded by a white noncommissioned officer, marched up Franklin Street. One of the soldiers stepped from the squad when it halted and took up position in front of the three-story brick home. The squad moved on. A curtain on one of the windows moved slightly. It was closed quickly.

3

At Twelfth and Broad streets "Uncle Simon," the Crump's butler, was chatting with several Yankee soldiers who had stopped their covered supply wagon in front of the house. One of the soldiers asked Simon how it felt to be free. When he said he had been free for more than a year, they were surprised.

The Yankee asked if Mr. Crump weren't a Confederate supporter.

"Yes, sir. He's in the Confederate Army."

"I'll be damned," said the Union soldier.

Simon asked about the contents of the wagon, and the soldiers disclosed that they were transporting food for the troops occupying the city. They climbed back on and the driver snapped the whip. As the wagon jerked forward, Simon reached over and grabbed a ham out of the back. He rapidly swung the meat behind his back and with his other hand waved goodbye to the soldiers. He then turned and slipped around the back of the Crump house and through the rear door.[2]

4

General Weitzel dismounted from his horse before the gray building at Twelfth and Clay streets. He walked up the front steps, followed by Major Stevens, and knocked. The door opened and Mrs. O'Melia showed the two men in, explaining that she was President Davis's housekeeper. She told them Mr. Davis had said to expect someone from the Union Army and welcomed the two men. General Weitzel thanked her and provided his assurance that Davis's property would be respected and protected. She was welcome to stay, he said.

5

Mrs. Pember followed the Confederate surgeon and the Union colonel as they inspected the injured and sick men.

When the colonel stopped at the bed of a soldier with a splintered and bandaged leg to examine the wound, the soldier drew back. Mrs. Pember assured the soldier that the Union colonel was a doctor and meant no harm. The Confederate doctor explained that the leg had been shattered by an exploding shell during the battle at Petersburg.

On his inquiry about the hospital's supply of morphine, the Union doctor was told that there was very little. Mrs. Pember relayed to the colonel the current count of Confederate sick and wounded.

"Not very many for such a large facility," mused the colonel.

Many had left when they heard the city was on the verge of being lost to the Union Army, explained Mrs. Pember. Some of them were "hospital rats," she started to explain. The colonel held up his hand to stop her. Union hospitals also had them, he said.

The two doctors and Mrs. Pember completed their rounds and returned to the surgeon's office in the receiving building. It was a small room with a wooden desk and three wooden chairs. A few books lined a shelf on one wall.

The Union colonel began the meeting by suggesting strongly that many of the patients be moved to Camp Jackson.

"What?" cried Mrs. Pember.

"Please, Mrs. Pember. Let the colonel finish," admonished the surgeon.

"I will not be quiet. These patients are not well enough to be moved. It would kill some of them," she said.

"Mrs. Pember," the Union colonel began. "We are not barbarians. We will take great care in moving them. I feel they would receive better care at Camp Jackson. It would free the staff here to treat the more seriously wounded."

Mrs. Pember stared defiantly at the colonel and the Confederate surgeon laughed.

"Are you a doctor, Mrs. Pember?" the Union colonel asked.

"No, colonel. I am not."

"Then, why don't you leave the medical decisions to us," the colonel replied.

"I know my patients. I have nursed them for three years. I don't need a doctor to tell me whether or not the patients are well enough to be moved," she countered.

"Lord, doctor! How do you put up with this woman?" the colonel asked the Confederate surgeon.

"Sometimes it is difficult, colonel. But I have to agree with her."

The Union doctor said he would pass their objections along, but that he would recommend that the patients be moved.[3]

6

The Union wagon train slowed on Main Street and then halted. The road ahead was blocked by burning debris, still falling from the buildings. The lead rider came back along the train telling the drivers they would divert to Broad Street. As he approached a wagon near the end of the train, one of the drivers pointed to a woman and her boys huddled in an adjacent field.

"They look petrified, sergeant."

The sergeant dismounted from his horse and approached the family. Removing his hat, he asked if they needed help. The boys moved closer to their mother, Rebecca Jane Allen.

The sergeant asked why they were sitting in the field. John pointed across it towards the burning building. The soldier asked if they lived there, but John shook his head and pointed to their house.

"I don't think you have to worry now. Looks like the fire is burning itself out," the soldier explained.

The sergeant looked around, uncomfortable at not getting any answer to his comment. He looked at Rebecca Jane.

"Ma'am? You need anything. Food? We can spare some."

The boys looked expectantly at their mother.

"We don't need no Yankee handouts. My husband will be home soon," she said, avoiding his eyes.

Shrugging his shoulders, the soldier put his hat back on, turned and returned to the wagon train. As it moved on, Rebecca Jane and the boys began to carry their possessions back to their house. The oldest boy balanced a chair on his head with the legs pointed skyward. Only he knew how vulnerable his mother was. While she rarely showed emotion, he had overheard her crying softly in her room one night after he had gone to bed.

7

Judith McGuire watched from her house as Union soldiers
marched through the street and others, off duty, walked around
becoming familiar with the city.

*The Federal soldiers were roaming about the streets;
either whiskey or the excess of joy had given some of them
the appearance of being beside themselves. We had hoped
that very little whiskey would be found in the city, as, by
order of the Mayor, casks were emptied yesterday evening
in the streets. . . . It soon became evident that protection
would be necessary for the residences, and at the request
of Colonel P. I went to the Provost Marshal's office to ask
for it. Mrs. P. was unfortunately in the country, and only
ladies were allowed to apply for guards. Of course this was
a very unpleasant duty, but I must undertake it. Mrs. D.
agreed to accompany me, and we proceeded to the City
Hall. . . . After passing through crowds of negro soldiers
there, we found on the steps some of the elderly gentlemen
of the city seeking admittance, which was denied them. I
stopped to speak to Mr.——, in whose commission house I
was two days ago, and saw him surrounded by all the
stores which usually make up the establishment of such a
merchant; it was now a mass of blackened ruins. He had
come to ask protection for his residence, but was not
allowed to enter. We passed the sentinel, and an officer
escorted us to the room in which we were to ask our
country's foe to allow us to remain undisturbed in our own
houses. Mrs. D. leant on me tremblingly; she shrank from
the humiliating duty. For my own part, though my heart
beat loudly and my blood boiled, I never felt more high
spirited or lofty than at that moment. A large table was
surrounded by officials, writing or talking to the ladies,
who came on the same mission that brought us. I approached the officer who sat at the head of the table, and
asked him politely if he was the Provost Marshal. "I am
the Commandant, madam," was the respectful reply.
"Then to whom am I to apply for protection for our
residence?"*
*"You need none, madam; our troops are perfectly
disciplined, and dare not enter your premises." "I am
sorry to be obliged to undeceive you, sir, but when I left*

home seven of your soldiers were in the yard of the residence opposite to us, and one has already been into our kitchen." He looked surprised, and said, "Then, madam, you are entitled to a guard. Captain, write a protection for the residence on the corner of First and Franklin Streets, and give these ladies a guard." This was quickly done, and as I turned to go out, I saw standing near me our old friend, Mrs.—. Oh! how my heart sank when I looked into her calm, sad face, and remembered that she and her venerable and highly esteemed husband must ask leave to remain in peace in their home of many years. The next person who attracted my attention was that sweet young girl, S.W. Having no mother, she of course must go and ask that her father's beautiful mansion may be allowed to stand uninjured. Tears rolled down her cheeks as she pressed my hand in passing. Other friends were there; we did not speak, we could not; we sadly looked at each other and passed on. Mrs. D. and myself came out, accompanied by our guard.[4]

As Mrs. McGuire and her friend left City Hall, another Richmond woman stomped up to the commandant and asked what "fool" had ordered a Negro soldier to stand guard in front of General Lee's home on Franklin Street. The commandant was surprised on hearing this and wrote out an order to have the guard replaced with a white soldier.

8

Mrs. McGuire's wasn't the only complaint to be heard that day. Nellie Grey protested about Union soldiers at the Arlington, a boarding house at Sixth and Main streets.

They were fully armed, and had come, as they said, to search the house for Rebels. The one who undertook to search our rooms came quite in and closed the door while his companions went below . . . Anxious to get rid of him quickly, I helped him in the search.

Going to the bed I threw the mattress over so he could see that no one was concealed beneath . . .

"There's nothing for you to find," I informed him. . . .

I led the way into the next room to be searched, he

following, asseverating in tipsy whispers. "Good Secesh
as you is, sis," every few minutes.
We found little Ruf Pagett cleaning his gun.
"Better hide that, sonny," said our friend, glancing
around. "That other fellow out there, he'll take it from
you. But I won't take it from you. I won't take nothin'. I'm
good Secesh as you is, bud. Hide your gun, bud."

Downstairs Nellie's friend, Mrs. Sampson, was having trouble with other Northern soldiers and threatening to report them
to General Weitzel. A Union officer resolved the problem,
however, saving Mrs. Sampson a trip to the General. A group
of Union soldiers quartered themselves under the veranda at
the double house that served as the Arlington, and no further
stragglers troubled the residents.[5]

9

Five-year-old George Lewis, the son of a freed slave who
lived in the Negro district north of Broad Street, told of his first
encounter with Union troops.

On the morning of April 3rd, there was so much noise and
excitement that my mother took me out of bed—changed
my night clothes, dressed me in my day ones—and started
with me out of the house. Just as we left the porch three or
four Yankee soldiers with guns on their shoulders stopped
us and told my mother that they wanted her to cook
breakfast for them . . . she turned around, took me in her
arms and returned to our house. I was frightened and hid
behind the kitchen door. After they finished eating the
cakes and fish, they got up from the table and took money
out of their pockets and paid my mother for the food and
for her trouble. These were Negro troops![6]

10

By evening the Union soldiers had made great headway in
fighting the fires in the business district. Blowing up buildings
along some streets, they had created breaks and contained the
fires.
Arriving home, Mrs. McGuire made notes in her diary.

The flames had decreased, but the business part of the city was in ruins. The second guard was soon posted [in front of her house], and the first carried off by the collar. Almost every house is guarded; and the streets are now . . . perfectly quiet. The moon is shining brightly on our captivity. . . .[7]

11

Constance Cary began a letter to her mother and brother from her attic room at her uncle's home, where she was helping his ill wife. She attempted to summarize the events of the past two days.

. . . My dearest mother.;
It is a special Providence that has spared you this! . . . Hardly had I seemed to dropped [sic] upon my bed that dreadful Sunday night—or morning rather—when I was wakened suddenly by four terrific explosions, one after the other, making the windows of my garret shake. . . . Soon the fire spread, shells in the burning arsenal began to explode, and a smoke arose that shrouded the whole town, shutting out every vestige of blue sky and April sunshine. Flakes of fire fell around us, glass was shattered, and chimneys fell. . . .

It was suggested that some of us should go to headquarters and ask, as our neighbors were doing, for a guard for the house where an invalid lay so critically ill. Edith and I were the volunteers for service, and set out for the Capitol Square, taking our courage in both hands. Looking down from the upper end of the square, we saw a huge wall of fire blocking out the horizon. In a few hours no trace was left of Main, Cary, and Canal Streets, from 8th to 18th Streets, except tottering walls and smoldering ruins. The War Department was sending up jets of flame. Along the middle of the streets smoldered a long pile, like street-sweepings, of papers torn from the different departments' archives of our beloved Government. . . .[8]

12

Kate Mason Rowland, working as a nurse at one of the Confederate hospitals, also recorded her impressions.

Such . . . long, long days . . . ! . . . Night is coming on.
The sky in the direction of Richmond is lurid with the glare
of burning houses. All day since early dawn the air has
been filled with shells bursting and columns of smoke and
flame ascending from the flaming magazines and gov-
ernment buildings. . . . It was as if a great battle were
going on around us. This has been done by our own
people. . . .[9]

13

The five officers stood beside their mounts below the south
portico of the Capitol building. The grounds around them were
bathed in a strange mixture of light from the moon and the glow
of the dying fires below the square. The displaced citizens on
the grounds and the Union soldiers encamped along the edge of
the square had settled down for the night.

The officers mounted their horses and set out onto Ninth
Street to inspect the city. They moved slowly through the sooty
air. As they approached Franklin Street, a soldier guarding the
burned-out shell of the Confederate War Department building
snapped to attention and saluted. General Weitzel returned the
salute. The riders turned west on Franklin Street. The beauty
and quiet of the well-kept, two- and three-story brick homes
stood in contrast to the devastation below the Capitol. Here
and there windows displayed candles, their lights flickering, but
many of the houses were dark. At each intersection and in front
of many of the houses stood sentries.

"The Lee home," General Wheeler said, pointing to the left.

The Union officers turned south at Sixth Street and rode
down the hill towards the river. At the corner of Main Street
they passed the Arlington House. Soldiers camped in front of
the building sat in small groups, some talking to boardinghouse
residents. At Canal Street the officers halted their horses.

"Tredegar Iron Works," said Wheeler, pointing to the
southwest. "It was spared major damage."

The view to the southeast and south was different. Smoke
rolled from the wooden beams that stretched between the
granite bases of the Richmond-Petersburg railroad bridge. Five
blocks downriver only the stone bases remained of Mayo's
Bridge. Flames still rose from the shell of the munitions arsenal
between Fourth and Seventh streets. In the moonlight the shell

of the Gallego Flour Mill stood as a stark monument to the conflagration.

Weitzel signaled for the group to move along Canal Street. The horses stepped carefully through the debris-littered street. At the Canal Basin near Ninth Street, Weitzel halted his men again. Looking north towards Shockoe Hill, he scanned the devastation. He shook his head, wondering aloud why anyone would give an order leading to this destruction.

"All right, gentlemen. We'll make a sweep through the remainder of the burned area and call it a night. There's lots to do tomorrow," said Weitzel.

He touched his boots to the side of his horse and the group moved on.[10]

14

Emmie Crump was the only one who had not retired after the nightly Bible reading. She sat at her desk writing a letter to her father, an ardent secessionist and assistant secretary of treasury.

Emmie recounted the days' events—the terrible explosions and fires; how the servants had saved their home from going up in flames three times by extinguishing burning embers landing on the roof; how the Yankee soldiers had passed their house on Broad Street; the dreadful sight of the Union flag being raised over the Capitol building; and the consternation caused by Peter.

"During that day when we were in much fear that the house would be taken possession of," she wrote, "Peter came in and said to mother in a most comforting manner: 'Don't you be scared, Miss May, I done tell 'em you is a good union woman!'

"The indignation this excited was so intense, we girls could scarcely be restrained from hanging a Confederate flag out of the window, to remove the shameful blot from our house and name. Poor, innocent Peter had no idea of the result of his little fabrication on mother," Emmie wrote.[11]

15

Dr. Hoge's wife also wrote a letter that night, telling her husband that the explosion of the arsenal had blown out all the windows in his beloved Second Presbyterian Church. The lecture room caught fire, but it was put out, she added, and though the roof of their house was covered with wet blankets and shawls, it caught fire three times.

> *. . . I made every arrangement to leave the house, each member of the household put on two sets of underclothes & two dresses & made up a bundle of clothing & took a snack & a bottle of milk & carried everything in the parlor. . . .*[12]

Lilian Cook added a note in her diary observing that Union soldiers had come to the Hoge house asking for food.

> *This morning a Federal came in the kitchen before breakfast for something to eat. Mrs. Hoge gave him something, then told him he had better leave, as she had orders from General Ripley that if any private entered the house, he must be reported. He said it was all right and left. Several colored troops have also been in for something to eat.*[13]

Elizabeth Van Lew also wrote in her diary the feelings she had about the arrival of the Union soldiers. "Oh Army of my country, how glorious was your welcome!"[14]

16

As night fell, Chimborazo Hospital was still under the direction of the Confederate doctors and Phoebe Pember. There were few sounds, save an occasional moan or snore, when matron Pember lay down and quickly drifted into a heavy and dreamless sleep in the small room adjoining the storage room.

Asleep less than an hour, she was abruptly awakened to the sounds of the storage room door being forced open. Phoebe sat up and listened to the muffled murmur of several voices. Without hesitating, she stood up, rapidly putting on her robe while checking the contents of its right pocket. She moved quickly across the room, throwing the door of the storage room open. Mrs. Pember came face to face with five rough looking men, all unshaven, red-eyed from drink and poorly clothed. She recognized them immediately; all were "hospital rats."

The leader was a burly man with whom she had had run-ins before.

Mrs. Pember later recalled, in vivid detail, the ensuing demands from the ringleader.

> *"We have come for the whiskey!"*
>
> *"You cannot and shall not have it!"*
>
> *"It don't belong to you."*
>
> *"It is in my charge, and I intend to keep it. Go out of my pantry; you are all drunk."*
>
> *"Boys," he said, "pick up that barrel and carry it down the hill. I will attend to her! . . ."*
>
> *"Wilson!" I said, "you have been in this hospital a long time. Do you think from what you know of me that the whiskey can be taken without my consent?"*
>
> *He became very insolent.*
>
> *"Stop that talk; your great friends have all gone, and we won't stand that now. Move out of the way!"*
>
> *He advanced towards the barrel, and so did I, only being in the inside, I interposed between him and the object of contention. The fierce temper blazed up in his face, and catching me roughly by the shoulder, he called me a name that a decent woman seldom hears and even a wicked one resents.*
>
> *Acting decisively . . . before he had time to push me one inch from my position, or to see what kind of an ally was in my hand, that sharp click, a sound so significant and so different from any other, struck upon his ear, and sent him back amidst his friends, pale and shaken. . . .*
>
> *"You had better leave . . . for if one bullet is lost, there are five more ready, and the room is too small for even a woman to miss six times. . . ."*
>
> *"You think yourself very brave now, but wait an hour; perhaps others may have pistols, too, and you won't have it entirely your way after all."*

The intruders backed out of the storage room and Mrs. Pember moved quickly to close the door tightly. She took the head off one of the flour barrels and nailed it across the door.[15]

19. *Fire sweeps across the Richmond business district and shells explode over the city as soldiers and citizens flee over Mayo's Bridge on April 3d. The scene is depicted in this Currier & Ives print.*

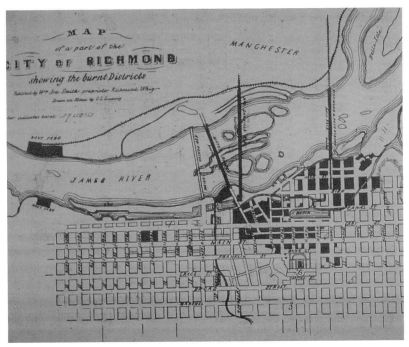

20. *Fire burned a major part of Richmond on April 3d and 4th (blacked out area), before the Union Army halted the devastation. Even Richmonders acknowledged that the Northern soldiers saved the city.*

21. *Confederate ironclads anchored below the city in the James River were blown up after the order came to evacuate Richmond.*

22. *Two Union cavalrymen climbed to the Capitol roof to raise the stars and stripes. Richmonders wept at the sight.*

23. *Richmonders fled to Capitol Square to seek a safe haven from the fires. Many persons escaped with only meager belongings. The air was so filled with smoke and ashes, it was difficult to breathe.*

24. Union soldiers march up Main Street April 3d as the city burns.

*25. Union soldiers stacked arms and camped on the lawn of Capitol Square.
Richmond's City Hall building on Broad Street is seen in the background.*

26. *Northern soldiers stand below and on the south portico of the state Capitol in this photograph taken on April 3d by one of Mathew Brady's photographers. Some writers have identified the photograph as recording the "official surrender" of the city with General Weitzel and Mayor Mayo standing on the portico. Magnification of the photograph, however, shows this is not correct.*

27. *After entering Richmond, Union soldiers were organized into fire brigades and halted the spread of blazes sweeping the business district.*

28. One of the saddest sights for Southerners was the Union flag flying over the state Capitol as shown in this photograph taken from the Kanawha Canal turning basin. Shells of burned-out buildings stand in the foreground.

29. Smoke rises from buildings on Bank Street in this view of the city taken from Capitol Square. Horses of the Union cavalry stand at the fence bordering the lower end of the square.

Tuesday, April 4

*B*EFORE the evacuation of Richmond began two days ago, the city's population numbered more than 100,000, including whites, Confederate soldiers, slaves and free blacks. It is difficult to estimate the numbers remaining, except to say that the Confederate soldiers and some whites are gone. In their place have come thousands of Union Army soldiers and their followers—prostitutes, carpetbaggers and other opportunity seekers.

Of those Richmonders who stayed, many have yet to venture from their homes for fear of Yankee soldiers, Confederate Army deserters and convicts who escaped from the penitentiary at Canal and Belvidere streets. Fears that women would be molested by Union soldiers have proven unfounded.

No one knows when the war will end, but there seems to be a general consensus that the cause is lost. Questions of survival are uppermost on the citizens' minds. How will Southerners be treated by occupying forces? What price will be demanded of Richmond citizens by Northern politicians?

Will freed blacks seek revenge for years of slavery?

Richmond! Oh, Richmond! Will your wounds ever heal?

9

GENERAL Weitzel sat at his desk reviewing dispatches from Grant's headquarters. Upon reading the latest message, he relayed orders to his aide to "to organize a police force, to start up the gas and water works and allow, quote, 'loyal landlords,' to open hotels and other establishments."[1]

2

The orderly walked up and gently touched Mrs. Pember on the shoulder to get her attention. The Yankee doctor had returned, he told her. She instructed him to finish changing the injured soldier's bandage and then hastened to the administration building. She crossed the bare ground between the buildings in quick steps. Her black, high-buttoned shoes sounded on the floor as she rushed down the hall to the chief surgeon's office.

The Union doctor smiled when Mrs. Pember entered, and told her he had good news, quickly disarming her. It seems his commander agreed with her and the Confederate surgeon. The wounded and ill prisoners should be left at Chimborazo Hospital for the time being.

Mrs. Pember thanked him for the news, but sat quietly.

"Is there something else you need, Mrs. Pember?" the Union officer asked.

"When are you going to place guards?"

"Do you think they are needed?"

"After last night, yes. Five hospital rats tried to take a barrel of whiskey. I scared them off with this," she said, revealing her pistol, which barely covered the palm of her hand.

"I didn't know you had a pistol," said the Confederate surgeon. He leaned across his desk to look closer.

"And such a large weapon," laughed the Union officer.

"It may be small, colonel, but it would make any man think twice about taking advantage of me. Even you."

"That it would," agreed the Confederate surgeon, grinning at the colonel.

"Would you really have used it?" asked the Union officer, but before she could answer, he replied to his own question. "Yes, I believe you would have."

Later one of the Union guards confided to Mrs. Pember that the federal chief surgeon had grown "awful afraid of her."[2]

3

The tall, thin man walked across the deck of the steamer, *River Queen*, at City Point near Petersburg. A young boy was at his side. From a distance the man looked remarkably like Jefferson Davis, but those watching knew he was not.

"We're ready, Mr. President," said Captain Bradford.*

The *River Queen* would follow the *Malvern*, Admiral David Porter's flagship, and a tug. Porter had ordered the James River cleared of Confederate torpedoes and now felt the waterway was safe. But Captain Bradford requested the president to stay on the upper deck during the trip where he would face less likelihood of being injured if the ship struck a submerged mine. Also along for the trip was Lincoln's personal guard, William H. Crook. The *River Queen* got underway about 9 A.M. and overtook the *Malvern* about an hour-and-a-half later.

4

Young Jennie D. Harrold carried a bag over her shoulder containing a new calico dress, a new alpaca dress and a wheat-colored straw hat. Under one arm she held her dog, Frank. With the city now under martial law, her family was returning to see what damage had befallen their Richmond home. They found their house being guarded by a teenaged soldier.

> *We had a boy about sixteen years of age from Brooklyn, who informed us that his name was Harry Bluff. He told us he was almost starved and we provided him with the best*

---

*No first name for Captain Bradford could be found in the official records. The numerous accounts of President Abraham Lincoln's trip to Richmond provide conflicting accounts as to whether the president was aboard the *River Queen* or the *Malvern*.

lunch we had, but he looked with wide open eyes and said,
"Do you think I would eat a thing you Rebs give me? Why,
you would poison me."[3]

5

Tad looked up to the wheelhouse from where his father was
calling for him. He ran up the stairs and went inside. His father,
Captain Bradford, and the wheelman stood gazing out the
windows.

"Up there. On top of the cliff. That's Drewry's Bluff. The
Confederates had their cannons up there, aimed down toward
the river. They could blow up a ship like this with one well-
placed shot," explained the captain, adding that the Union
soldiers now had control of the fort.

Captain Bradford pointed to the north bank where the
remains of several Confederate ships stuck out of the water.
The Confederates blew them up Sunday night, he explained.
Dead horses and broken military ordnance floated downriver.

The *River Queen* slowly passed the one-hundred-foot high
bluff. The cliff was commanding, in contrast to the low land on
the right. The river was nearing low tide, exposing the giant
roots of hardwood trees that lined the right bank. The landscape was beautiful this time of year as new leaves greened the
area. An osprey circled overhead looking for a fish or water
snake in the river below.

It was unusually warm for the season, but the breeze created
by the movement of the ship provided some relief for the
president and Tad. Just after they passed Drewry's Bluff, the
River Queen and the *Malvern* had to anchor because there was
too much debris in the river to proceed farther.[4]

6

The woman referred to as "Agnes" ventured out from the
Spottswood Hotel after convincing a "lad" to accompany her.
As the two walked up Franklin Street, they saw the Union
soldier pacing back and forth in front of General Lee's house.
Agnes's first reaction was indignation, but then she recalled,
"presently the door opened, the guard took his seat on the
steps and proceeded to investigate the contents of a very neatly

furnished tray, which Mrs. Lee in the kindness of her heart had
sent out to him.''

She later wrote her friend, Mrs. Pryor, in Petersburg.

> *I am obliged to acknowledge that there is really no hope
> now of our ultimate success. Everybody says so. My heart
> is too full for words. General Johnston* says we may
> comfort ourselves by the fact that war may decide a
> policy, but never a principle. I imagine our principle is all
> that remains to us of hope or comfort.*[5]

7

After a conference President Lincoln and Tad were transferred to a barge that was towed up the river by the tug,
Glance. On board the tug was a detachment of 30 marines.
About a mile below Richmond the tug ran aground and the
barge had to be rowed to shore near Rocketts Landing. A large
group of blacks had already gathered on the dock as the
entourage arrived. Lincoln, Porter and Crook searched the crowd
and beyond for a welcoming party of soldiers. The president
remained calm. He took off his famous stovepipe hat and
waved it. The people on shore cheered.

"Let's go ashore, admiral," he said finally.

The presidential party stepped ashore surrounded by several
marines carrying carbines. The president questioned the neces-
sity for protection, but Admiral Porter said the guards were a
precaution against any potential animosity the white population
might have.

The crowd of blacks pushed to the edge of the dock and
repeatedly called out "God Bless our liberator." Young Tad
moved closer to his father. He had never seen such a sea of
black faces. A man ran forward and knelt, taking the president's hand and kissing it. The armed sailors moved closer and
the president told the man not to kneel before him.

"That is not right. You must kneel to God only, and thank
him for the liberty you will hereafter enjoy," said Lincoln.[6]

Admiral Porter scanned the dock again, but neither Weitzel
nor any of his soldiers were to be seen.

"We'll walk," said Lincoln.

---

*General Joseph E. Johnston

"It's a long way, Mr. President."

"I'm used to long walks, admiral."[7]

The crowd split as the presidential party started forward. It crossed the dock and started up River Road. Several blacks in the crowd ran ahead to shout the president's arrival to all they encountered. The group crossed the wooden bridge over Bloody Run and walked up the hill. Where the road became Main Street, Lincoln halted the group for his first close view of Richmond since its capture. Two- and three-story homes and shops lined the street as it dipped down toward Shockoe Bottom and then rose again near the burned-out business district. As the group moved again a voice cried out.

"It's President Davis. Hang him!" shouted a black man from a tree.

"No!" yelled someone below. "That's President Lincoln!"

"I knows President Davis when I see him, and that be him," the man in the tree argued.

Two members of the honor guard ran to the tree.

"Hang him!" the black man shouted again.

A friend below explained the man was drunk. Ordering the man out of the tree, the guards told his friend to take him home or he would be arrested.[8]

President Lincoln fanned his face with his hat. Perspiration dribbled down everyone's faces, leaving small smears on the skin where dust kicked up by the crowd had settled. The presidential group moved toward the city, joined by more and more blacks, many trying to touch the president.

Admiral Porter leaned toward President Lincoln and yelled over the noise that the building on the left was Libby Prison. The group stopped. Lincoln explained to his son that the prison had held hundreds of Union officers until the Confederates fled Richmond. It was considered one of the worst prisons in the South and now held captured Confederate soldiers and deserters.

"Pull it down," yelled a black man.

"Tear it down!" shouted another.

Lincoln turned and faced the crowd.

"No! Leave it as a monument." he said.[9]

The crowd of blacks became larger and more vocal. The people poured in "so fearfully that I thought we all stood a chance of being crushed to death," noted Porter, who ordered his men to fix bayonets. But Lincoln sought to calm the situation. He began to speak:

"My poor friends, you are free—free as air. You can cast off the name of slave and trample upon it; it will come to you no more. Liberty is your birthright."

The crowd roared at the words and it was with difficulty that the presidential party edged its way toward the city.[10]

8

Peter came quietly through the back of the Crump house. He looked like a child with a secret. He walked to the front of the house.

"Where have you been, Peter?" asked Emmie.

"Around. Seeing what the Yankees doing."

"You know something, don't you. I can tell."

"No, Miss."

Peter looked down at the floor.

"Don't tell your mother, but President Lincoln's here."

"Where?"

"He be coming up Twelfth Street in a few minutes. I saw him and the crowd turning from Main Street."

Emmie ran up the stairs and into Kate Tabb's room. The windows there, which faced the back and side of the house, gave views of Twelfth Street.

"What are you doing?" asked Kate.

"Shh! I'm trying to see President Lincoln."

Kate jumped off her bed and ran to the window. They could see the crowd wending its way up the street.

"There he is, between the marines," cried Emmie.

"He sure is ugly, isn't he," giggled Kate. "Look at his nose."

"Let's go downstairs. Maybe we can sneak out of the house."

The two girls ran down the hall, then slowed to a normal walk and trod quietly down the stairs. Near the bottom they saw Peter and Simon whispering at the front door. Simon held the door ajar.

"Someone at the door?" asked Mrs. Crump, coming from the parlor.

"No, Ma'am. Heard a noise. Everything's okay though."

Mrs. Crump listened. "There is a noise. It sounds like a large crowd of people. What is it, Peter?"

"President Lincoln is here. He's walking up Twelfth Street."

"Oh. I should have guessed."

Mrs. Crump turned and went back into the parlor.[11]

9

The crowd greeting President Lincoln as he proceeded to the Confederate White House was mostly black. Mrs. McGuire noted the white reaction, "Our people were in nothing rude or disrespectful; they only kept themselves away from a scene so painful." She described the reception "so feeble from the motley crew of vulgar men and women, that the Federal officers themselves, I suppose, were ashamed of it. . . ."[12]

10

The reception was also reported by correspondent Chester.

The colored population was wild with enthusiasm. Old men thanked God in a very boisterous manner, and old women shouted upon the pavement as high as they had ever done at a religious revival. . . . Every one declares that Richmond never before presented such a spectacle of jubilee. It must be confessed that those who participated in this informal reception of the President were mainly negroes. There were many whites in the crowd, but they were lost in the great concourse of American citizens of African descent. Those who lived in the finest houses either stood motionless upon their steps or merely peeped through the window blinds.[13]

11

The president and Tad continued in the "parade" across the wide, dirt Broad Street, a cloud of dust in their wake. "Wherever it was possible for a human being to find a foothold there was some man or woman or boy straining his eyes after the President," wrote Crook.[14] They walked two blocks up Twelfth Street to Clay Street and Mr. Davis's mansion. Lincoln stopped at the street corner, removed his hat and wiped his brow, noticing his son's flushed face. As they stood on the mansion porch, the president turned and waved to the crowd one more time before entering.

Chester made these additional notes on the scene to be telegraphed later to his newspaper in Pennsylvania.

> *General Weitzel received the President upon the pavement, and conducted him up the steps. General Shepley, after a good deal of trouble, got the crowd quiet and introduced Admiral Porter, who bowed his acknowledgments for the cheering with which his name was greeted. The President and party entered the mansion . . ., the crowd still accumulating around it.*[15]

Lincoln sank in a chair, looking "pale and haggard, utterly worn out," noted John S. Barnes, captain of the *Malvern*, who also had accompanied the president.

"I wonder if I could get a glass of water?" asked Lincoln.

The staff officers took seats around the parlor as Lincoln, his son, Barnes, Crook and Admiral Porter refreshed themselves near one of the south windows. The high ceiling helped to keep the room cool. The endless cheers and yells of the crowd outside could be heard inside.[16]

10

ALLAS Tucker stood on the edge of the crowd gathered at the Davis Mansion. From a distance the youngster watched a man seated on a stone wall opposite the house. He held a pad in one hand and drew with the other. Dallas walked over behind the man and watched over his shoulder. In quick motions the artist sketched the entire scene.

"You one of those newspaper artists?" Dallas asked.

"*Frank Leslie's Illustrated Newspaper.*"

"That's good. You been drawing scenes of the battles too?"

"Yes, I've been at the battles."

The illustrator's work showed the Davis Mansion in the background, the north side of the house in shadow. Three trees stood in front of the house, a black person in each one. The street in front was filled with blacks and soldiers, many with an arm raised, their mouths wide open in shouts of joy. The illustration so perfectly captured the scene that Dallas could almost hear shouts and cheers emanating from the paper.

2

Rumors about the fate of Lee's army ran through Richmond. DeLeon noted some in his journal.

> *Clinging, with the tenacity of the drowning, to the least stray of hope, they would not yet give up utterly that army they had looked on so long as invincible—that cause, which was more than life to them! Though they knew the country around was filled with deserters and stragglers; though the Federals had brigades lying round Richmond in perfect idleness—still for a time the rumor gained credit that General Lee had turned on his pursuer at Amelia Court House, and gained a decisive victory over him.*[1]

It was a false hope.

About the same time Lincoln was resting at the Confederate White House, the gray-and-white-bearded general walked toward the train standing on the rail siding outside the town of Amelia, about 30 miles southwest of Richmond. Several junior staff officers walked a few steps behind him. General Lee reached out and pulled back the tarpaulin from one of the cars. Before them were crates of dull metal and wood—crates of ammunition. The general said nothing. He went to the next car and pulled back another tarpaulin. Again the car was filled with ammunition.

The general turned away and started back across the field. Before him were several thousand men with drawn faces and empty stomachs, standing in small groups. Others had fallen on the ground to rest. Still others stood in staggered formations—a last valiant effort to resemble an army. They hadn't eaten for days and now their general was unable to feed them, despite telegrams sent to Richmond before the evacuation requesting food supplies.

"His face was still calm, as it always was, but his carriage was no longer erect, as his soldiers had been used to see[ing] it," a junior staff officer, George Cary Eggleston, wrote later.

"The troubles of those last days had already plowed great furrows in his forehead. His eyes were red as if with weeping; his cheeks sunken and haggard; his face colorless. No one who looked upon him then, as he stood there in full view of the disastrous end, can ever forget the intense agony written upon his features."[2]

3

President Lincoln set down his glass and wiped his mouth with the cotton napkin. Then he jumped up.

"Let's go. Come, let's look at the house!" he said with a boyish grin.[3]

On the way out of the parlor he requested Weitzel to round up a few prominent Richmonders to meet with him later. Weitzel nodded and delegated the details to Major Stevens. The group went up the winding staircase to the second floor. Lincoln leaned into the small room, which, Weitzel explained, had been the office of Davis's secretary, Burton Harrison. The group proceeded to Davis's former office. An American flag rested in one corner where the Confederate flag had stood two days before. Lincoln walked around the desk and sat down. He put his hands on the desk and felt the wood. He looked around the room and leaned back in the chair. He seemed to be imagining how his adversary would have looked at the desk.[4]

The president got up and offered his son a seat. Lincoln dwarfed all those around him when he stood.

"Mr. President, Judge Campbell is waiting in the parlor and General Anderson of Tredegar is on his way," reported Major Stevens.

"Thank you, major. We will be with them shortly. General, let's see the rest of the house while we wait for the other gentleman to arrive," the president said.

4

Judge John A. Campbell, a bearded man in his sixties, sat uneasily on a Victorian chair in the parlor. As assistant secretary of war, he was the only official representative of the Confederate government remaining in the city. He felt mixed emotions. A Southerner by birth, he stood behind the principle of states' rights, but he knew in his heart his side had lost. Now he was about to meet with the leader of the victors. A year earlier he had seen Lincoln at Hampton Roads during an unsuccessful meeting to seek ways to end the war. And before that Campbell had seen Lincoln in Washington.

Voices outside the parlor door interrupted his thoughts. The door opened.

"General Anderson, please wait in here. The president will be with you shortly. I believe you know Judge Campbell."

"Thank you, major."

Anderson shook hands with Campbell and took a seat. The door closed. Major Stevens paced in the front hallway off the parlor. He stopped upon hearing voices and footsteps on the staircase. Stevens tapped softly on the parlor door to warn Campbell and Anderson, and then opened the door.

"Mr. President, Judge Campbell and General Anderson," introduced Stevens.

"Gentlemen, thank you for coming. Please sit down," said the president.

The sound of Lincoln's voice trailed off as Stevens closed the door.[5]

5

The crowd outside the mansion continued to grow as word spread of Lincoln's arrival in the city. The scene had become much like a revival. People danced and sang black spirituals and some of the black Union soldiers joined in the celebration. Among the observers were several reporters from Northern and foreign newspapers. Edward A. Pollard, his own Richmond newspaper destroyed by the fire, was an observer and guide for the other correspondents.

6

Hundreds of blacks and whites gathered in other parts of the city also. However, they had another interest—the quest for food. They crowded the Capitol grounds, street corners and the steps of the City Hall.

"Please!" pleaded a woman to a soldier at Eighth and Grace streets. "Do you know where we can find food?"

The soldier looked at the woman, his response uncertain at first. Until now white women in Richmond had turned up their noses at him and the other soldiers. He glanced down at the pleading eyes of the five-year-old girl with the woman. He unslung his rifle and rested it against the iron fence. Then he unbuckled a pouch on his belt and took out two pieces of rations and handed them to the woman.

"Here. It's all the food I've got now."

"Thank you and God bless you. God bless you!"

As the mother and girl walked on, a small boy ran up to the soldier, holding out his hands.

"Me, too! Me, too!"

"I don't have no more. Sorry, boy." [6]

7

A few blocks away at the Spottswood Hotel, a well-dressed man closed the snaps of the saddle bag on his horse. A frequent visitor to the city, he had come too late to retrieve his money from one of the banks. He had money in many southern financial institutions, and he was preparing to leave for another town. The man put his boot into his horse's left stirrup and swung himself up. The call of a familiar voice stopped him from ordering the horse on.

"Mr. Frank! Mr. Frank! Please wait!"

A balding man ran up to the rider.

"Oh, God, I'm glad I found you."

"Trenton! I thought you would have left the city."

The man explained that he and his wife couldn't get away; it was too dangerous.

"What can I do for you?" asked the rider.

"My daughter. You must help me get her back to Richmond."

"Where is she?"

"North Carolina. I fear she will be made a prisoner. I would gladly give all I have to get her home."

The horseman considered the proposal.

"Please, Mr. Frank. If anyone can do it, you can. You've run the blockades. You've been through the lines countless times. You told me yourself."

"Yes, but keep your voice down. That's not something I want heard by the Yankees. North Carolina, you say."

"Yes, just below the border, near South Hill."

"If you pay in gold, I will have your daughter here in two days."

"Here!" said Trenton, holding up a small rawhide bag. "There are a few gold coins, my wife's wedding ring, some jewelry."

"I'll be back in two days, if not sooner," the rider said.

He started to urge his horse on, then paused and reached into the bag. He handed the wedding ring back to Trenton.

"God speed, Mr. Frank. God speed!"[7]

8

President Lincoln thanked the two men for coming, and said he would advise General Weitzel of his decisions on the points discussed. Afterwards as Campbell walked down the street, he thought back to the meeting. The president seemed to have only one goal—ending the war as soon as possible in order to restore peace. Campbell had suggested that the revocation of the ordinance of secession by the Virginia legislature would allow the state to start rebuilding as a member of the Union. He had urged moderation in the treatment of the South. "I spoke to him particularly for Virginia, and urged him to consult . . . with her public men . . . as to the restoration of peace."[8]

The judge had just reached the Capitol grounds when he heard the commotion behind him. A black man ran by shouting that President Lincoln was coming. Those camping on the grounds reacted slowly, fearing to go far from their temporary homes and meager belongings.

The carriage passed Campbell and turned into the square. Lincoln rode with his son, Admiral Porter, Generals Weitzel and Shepley. Crook rode alongside on a horse. As the carriage neared the south portico of the Capitol, a crowd quickly formed around the vehicle. It was composed mostly of black men and women welcoming their savior. There were, though, other shouts—"We need food!"

The president stood up in the carriage and waved to the crowd. He turned and gazed on the building Thomas Jefferson had designed, and whispered something in his son's ear. Tad looked up at the building.

The cries became louder for food, and as others in the crowd took up the chant, the escorting soldiers formed a ring around the carriage. After a brief discussion, Lincoln requested that General Weitzel ensure the speedy distribution of food and other supplies to the needy. He then stood for a brief period and waved to the crowd.

As the president sat back down, the carriage driver snapped the whip and the vehicle moved off slowly, the soldiers clearing people from its path. The carriage left the Capitol grounds and proceeded onto Ninth Street.

9

Sallie Ann Brock later wrote of the scene as the president toured the city and returned to Rocketts Landing.

All along his triumphal passage, sable multitudes of both sexes and every age gathered and pressed around the vehicle to press or kiss his hand, or to get a word or look from him. As the carriage rolled up the streets they ran after it in furious excitement, and made the welkin ring with the loud and continuous cheering peculiar to their race.[9]

Correspondent Chester reported that one black woman exclaimed: "I know that I am free, for I have seen Father Abraham and felt him."[10]

As the day neared its end, the carriage arrived back at Rocketts Landing where the president, tired but smiling, boarded the barge to be rowed back to the *Malvern*. Before the barge left the landing, General Weitzel asked what should be done with those captured. Lincoln looked toward the setting sun for a few moments, and then turned to the general.

"If I were in your place, I'd let 'em up easy. Let 'em up easy."[11]

10

The presidential party was not the only group to travel up the James River from City Point to Richmond, noted DeLeon.

> . . . *sutlers, peddlers and hucksters swarmed in like locusts, on the very first steamers up the river. They crowded Broad Street, the unburned stores of Main, and even the alleyways, with great piles of every known thing that could be put up in tin. They had calculated on a rich harvest; but they had reckoned without their host. There was no money in Richmond to spend with them; and after a profitless sojourn, they took up their tin cans, and one by one returned North—certainly wiser and, possibly better men. It was peculiar to note the universality of southern sympathy among these traders. There was scarcely one among them who didn't think the war "a darned shame;" they were intensely sympathetic and all came from south of the Pennsylvania line. . . .* [12]

11

At the Arlington, Mrs. Sampson heard the Union soldiers were giving away food. Her own hunger pangs gave her enough reason to swallow momentarily her hate for the enemy. Nellie Grey recorded Mrs. Sampson's sojourn to get some of the food.

> *"I'll take anything I can get out of the Yankees!" She exclaimed. "They haven't had any delicacy of feeling in taking everything we've got! I'm going for rations!"*
>
> *So Mrs. Sampson nerved herself up to the point where*

she took quite a pleasure and pride in her mission. But not so with the rest of us. It was a bitter pill, hard, hard to swallow. Mother, to whose lot some species of martyrdom was always falling, elected to go with Mrs. Sampson. So forth sallied these old Virginia matrons to "draw rations from the Yankees." However, once on our way to humiliation we began to console ourselves with thoughts of loaves and fishes. We would have enough to eat—sugar and tea and other delights! Presently mother and Mrs. Sampson returned, each with a dried codfish! There was disappointment and there was laughter. As each stately matron came marching in, holding her codfish at arm's length before her, Delia McArthur and I fell into each other's arms laughing. Besides the codfish, they each had a piece of fat, strong bacon about the size of a handkerchief folded once, and perhaps an inch thick. Now, we had no meat for a great while, and we were completely worn out with dried apples and peas, so we immediately set about cooking our bacon. Having such a great dainty and rare luxury, we felt ourselves in a position to invite company to dinner. Mrs. Sampson invited half of the household to dine with her, and we invited the other half. Soon there was a great sputtering and a delicious smell issuing from the Sampsons' apartment and from ours. . . .

As for the codfish, we had immediately hung that out of the window. The passer-by in the street below could behold it, dangling from its string, a melancholy and fragrant codfish. From Mrs. Sampson's window just below ours hung another melancholy codfish just like the one above it. . . .[13]

30. *General Godfrey Weitzel commanded the Union forces occupying Richmond.*

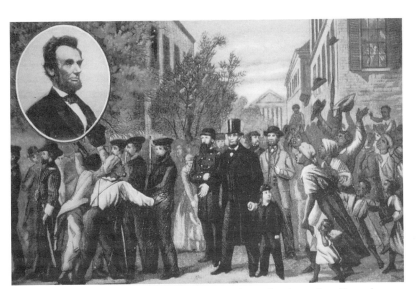

31. *When Weitzel had failed to meet Lincoln at Rocketts Landing, the president walked to the Davis Mansion, a distance of more than two miles.*

32. *After meeting with Judge John A. Campbell and Joseph Anderson, Lincoln, his son and Union officers left the Davis Mansion for a tour of Richmond.*

33. *Union soldiers stand on a wrecked railroad engine at a burned-out station April 4th, 1865. President Davis fled the city by train the night of April 2d.*

34. Only shells of buildings remained in Richmond's business district after the fire. The blaze was started by Confederate soldiers carrying out orders to burn the tobacco warehouses during the early hours of April 3d.

35. In this rarely seen photograph, Union cavalrymen ride up Franklin Street near the Lee House. Mrs. Lee, suffering from arthritis, was still there with her daughter, Mildred.

36. *General Robert E. Lee, aboard his horse, Traveller, returned to Richmond April 15th. Crowds of Richmonders, Union soldiers and some blacks stood silently along the streets as he made his way home.*

37. *Richmond, April 4, 1865. This view shows the devastated city as seen from Gamble's Hill. Federal forces occupied the city for five years, appointing the mayor and governor.*

38. *In the same view as the top photograph, Richmond today is a city of tall, modern buildings. The building at left is part of the Ethyl Corporation Headquarters. The building at right is the Federal Reserve Bank.*

39. *The rebuilt Richmond-Petersburg Railroad Bridge is shown in this 1871 drawing by Harry Fenn. The bridge was destroyed by fire a second time in 1882. In the background is the rebuilt city of Richmond.*

40. *In a similar view to the top photograph, the modern Manchester Bridge is shown crossing the James River from South Richmond to Ninth Street. The two buildings in the center form the James River Plaza.*

41. Published here for the first time is an allegorical sketch of the expiring Confederacy. The drawing was found on the mantel of the first floor, northeast room of the Davis Mansion April 3d, 1865. Along with it was the calling card of the French consul, Alfred Paul.

Saturday, April 15

*I*T has been 12 days since the Union Army occupied Richmond. The animosity between our Southern citizens and the Northern occupying forces has lessened. The Union soldiers have been courteous throughout, and now the citizens seem to be responding in like manner. The situation reminds one of soldiers in the field, where hate for the enemy can be mustered before and during battle. Facing each other during lulls, which sometimes lasted weeks, soldiers of the opposing forces traded coffee and tobacco, epithets and jokes. The common bond of being American, and in some cases, related by blood, led to familiarity.

Word of three important events has reached the city. General Lee surrendered the Army of Northern Virginia at Appomattox six days ago. The surrender has been confirmed by telegram. The end to the fight can not be far away. President Davis and his cabinet have left Danville, Virginia, and established a new headquarters in Greensboro, North Carolina.

The other news is not yet confirmed. Rumors are spreading that President Lincoln was shot last night in Washington and perhaps fatally wounded.

11

THE horseman reached the crest of Shockoe Hill. His uniform was wet from the spring rain. He turned and rode slowly west, his face and clothes stained from travel, his body weary and thin from little rest and meager food. The horse stopped, unable to go farther. The rider slumped in the saddle and the reins dropped from his hands.

Several persons ran from their porches to the man. Two women stared from behind an iron fence in front of their house. They went to the gate and opened it. They began to walk towards the soldier, then to run.

"Oh, God! It's Tom."

The rider slowly raised his head and looked at them.

"Tom! Tom!"

The soldier blinked, as if waking from sleep.

"I am home, mother. It's over."

The women reached to steady him as he slid from the saddle and stood weakly against his horse. They grabbed him in an embrace and sobbed.

DeLeon recorded the scene:

> The young soldier was surrounded; fair faces quivering with suspense. . . . [His] broad chest heaved as if it would burst, a great sob shook the stalwart frame, and a huge teardrop rolled down the cheek that had never changed color in the hottest flashes of the fight. And then the sturdy soldier—conquering his emotion but with no shame for it—told all he could and lightened many a heavy heart. And up to his own door they walked by his side . . . and there they left him alone to be folded in the embrace of the mother to whom he still was "glorious in the dust."[1]

2

Along the Lynchburg Road south of the city, weaponless Confederate soldiers straggled towards Richmond in groups of twos and threes, some hobbling with the aid of tree branches. They struggled the last few miles, fighting exhaustion with thoughts of loved ones and home. Privates, sergeants, lieutenants, walking one after another. Rank meant nothing now. Most still wore their uniforms, the only clothes they had. Every now and then a lucky officer who still had his horse rode by in a gallop. The nearness of the city drew the weary riders and pedestrians on.

Union soldiers in covered supply wagons slowly passed the Confederate soldiers. Some of the Union men stared at the men in their diminished state but spoke no unkind words. If the war had ended differently, the fate of the Confederates could have been their own. From a few of the wagons which were stopped along the way, drivers offered the soldiers a drink of water and a ration of codfish.

"I hear he's coming," the Union soldier said to a returning Confederate.

"He passed me an hour ago," replied the other.

3

Two Union guards stood at ease at the south end of the pontoon bridge, watching several supply wagons proceed toward Richmond from Manchester. They talked of family and home cooking—a roast, potatoes and gravy, peas and onions.

Home for one was Little Washington, Pennsylvania. The other said he lived not far from there in Butler. The first one spoke longingly of how he would love to walk up North Main Street in Little Washington and see his Pa and Ma, Sis . . . all waiting for him on the front porch.

A black soldier with them said nothing. He was looking south. His mouth dropped open and he raised his hand and pointed. Riding slowly towards them were several Confederate officers. The lead horseman had a gray-white beard and rode a magnificent looking white horse with a black mane and tail. People along the town's street stopped what they were doing and watched. The men took off their hats. No one spoke.

The black soldier turned and looked across the pontoon bridge toward the city. He started off in a jog, then a run. At Mayo's Island in the middle of the river, he passed several more Union soldiers.

"He's coming!" he shouted.

He ran on, crossing the northern section of the bridge and on to Fourteenth Street. "He's coming," he repeated to other soldiers and citizens along the way. He slowed his run. Something was unusual. People were lining the street up to the corner and on Main Street.

"They must already know," he thought.

He walked another block, looking at the faces of the people. They were expressionless. Most were white with the exception of a few black faces. Some of his fellow soldiers were waiting along with the citizens. He stopped, turned and looked back down the street and across the bridge. The horsemen were crossing Mayo's Island. The black soldier walked over to the side of the street and joined the expectant crowd.

4

"Here comes the general," whispered Rebecca Jane Allen as she stooped beside her youngest son. "Don't he look gallant."

Her oldest boy jumped to attention and saluted. His brothers did the same. As the general passed Fourteenth and Canal streets, he bowed his head slightly in acknowledgement of the onlookers waiting along the street.

Rebecca's youngest asked if his father were with the general. He would be home soon, she assured him. Maybe he was not far behind the general, she added. Then she was quiet.

"He is coming, isn't he, Ma?" asked the oldest boy.

5

The general rode slowly up Fourteenth Street, passing Cary Street, the original site of the state Capitol. It was there that his father had served as a state assemblyman. The pinch-faced civilians watched as the general passed the blackened remains of buildings on Main Street. As he neared Capitol Square, across from where his command had begun four years earlier, the crowd became larger. The line of people extended around the bottom of the square and west up Franklin Street. Hundreds of burned-out buildings formed the backdrop.

Young and old, prominent and common people. The Crump family, General Anderson, Judges Lyons and Campbell, Mayor Mayo, Dr. Minnigerode from St. Paul's and a priest from the

Catholic Cathedral.* Mrs. Simpson and Nellie Grey, John Leyburn, Connie Cary, Pollard, Chester and DeLeon. Servants to the families living in the homes along the street. And young Dallas Tucker. Nearly all of Richmond, and all were silent.

The general's horse turned the corner onto Franklin Street. The other four horsemen dropped back and he rode on alone, standing tall in the saddle. He focused his gaze straight ahead. It was so quiet that the *clip, clop, clip, clop* of Traveller's feet could be heard as the horse kicked up dirt from the street.

The general and his horse slowly moved past the corner of Eighth Street. Midway in the next block, he turned the horse to the front of the three-story brick house. Dismounting, he wrapped the reins around the iron post and walked up the steps to the porch, pausing at the door and turning to the crowd. He lifted his hat and bowed his head slightly.

Then General Robert E. Lee went into the house. "His people," DeLeon later wrote, "had seen him for the last time in his battle harness."[2]

---

*Now St. Peter's Catholic Church.

EPILOGUE

*F*OR five years after the war ended, Richmond was under Union control. Within weeks of Lee's surrender, hundreds of Confederate soldiers had come to the Richmond Capitol, most to swear allegiance to the Union, but some never would.

The city held its first Fourth of July celebration in 1871. The national holiday had gone virtually unobserved in the city since its occupation because of "bitterness and grief . . . so poignant and widespread that the people couldn't bring themselves to hold elaborate ceremonies based on the concept of national unity," wrote historian Virginius Dabney. Gradually the city recovered from its wounds, however, and rebuilt and prospered under the leadership of Joseph Bryan, Lewis Ginter and James H. Dooley, all former Confederate officers.

Life changed greatly for those who lived through the four days recorded in this book. Following is an encapsulation of what happened to some of those persons.

MRS. ROBERT C. STANARD moved to Washington, D.C., where she became a popular hostess. PHOEBE PEMBER relocated to Georgia and wrote *A Southern Woman's Story, Life in Confederate Richmond*. She also traveled frequently in America and abroad. She died in Pittsburgh in 1913.

CONSTANCE "CONNIE" CARY was in love with BURTON HARRISON, President Davis's secretary. She went to New Jersey after the war and for many months had no news of her beloved, who was captured with Davis. Learning he was imprisoned, she and her family worked for his release and the two were married in 1867. They moved to New York state where she began a career writing novels, plays and essays. Her book, *Recollections Grave and Gay*, tells of her life in Richmond during the war. She died in 1920, 16 years after her husband.

THOMAS COOPER DELEON also went on to a writing career, as did JOHN BEAUCHAMP JONES. Among DeLeon's works were *Four Years in Rebel Capitals* and *Belles, Beaux and Brains of the 60's*. Jones wrote a two-volume account entitled *A Civil War Clerk's Diary at the Confederate States Capital*.

THOMAS MORRIS CHESTER worked for the rights of blacks after the Civil War, traveling throughout the country, England and to Liberia, from which many of the slaves had come, promoting his ideas. He felt the war's end presented an opportunity for both races to compete on equal footing. He died a disillusioned man in 1892.

JOSEPH R. ANDERSON gained permission from the Federal occupying forces to start up Tredegar Iron Works two years after the war ended. As president of the company, he helped rebuild Richmond. He remained with the iron works for more than 20 years, nursing it along through good and bad times. He died in 1892.

RICHARD STODDERT "DICK" EWELL was captured at Sailor's Creek, Virginia, April 6, 1865, and imprisoned for about four months. After his release, he moved to his farm near Spring Hill, Tennessee. He died there of pneumonia in 1872.

GODFREY WEITZEL was relieved of duty less than two weeks after entering Richmond for failing to enforce an order that a prayer for President Lincoln be said at Richmond churches. He left the army in 1866 and joined the Army Corps of Engineers working on river and harbor improvements. He died in 1884 at the age of 49.

RAPHAEL SEMMES met harsh treatment from the federals. Although paroled at the end of the war, he was arrested in Mobile, Alabama, soon after and held prisoner in Washington, D.C., charged with having violated "the usage of war in escaping from the *CSS Alabama*." The ship in question was Semmes's flagship and was sunk by the *USS Kearsarge* June 19, 1864, off Cherbourg, France, where the *Alabama* was waiting to be overhauled. In the fall of 1866 Semmes accepted a chair of moral philosophy and English literature at Louisiana State University, but was forced from that position by political pressure before the end of the school year. He then became editor of the Memphis, Tennessee, *Daily Bulletin*, but was hounded out of that job by Northern foes. He finally retired to Mobile, Alabama, where he practiced law until he died in 1877 at the age of 68.

The REV. MOSES D. HOGE remained pastor of Second Presbyterian Church until his death in 1899. The REV. CHARLES MINNIGERODE continued his work as an Episcopal leader with the Episcopal Diocese of Virginia. He died in 1894.

WILLIAM "EXTRA BILLY" SMITH, who earned his nickname

because of his ability to get more from people and government officials than they were first willing to give, retired to his farm, "Monterosa," near Warrenton, Virginia. At the age of 80 he was elected to the Virginia House of Delegates and served two years. He died at 90, the father of 11 children.

JOSEPH CARRINGTON MAYO was reappointed mayor two months after the surrender of Richmond by the provisional governor and remained in office until May 4, 1868. He retired to New Kent County, Virginia, and lived there until his death on August 10, 1872. He was 78.

ELIZABETH VAN LEW was named postmistress of Richmond by President Grant and served two terms. After Grant left office, she was appointed a clerk in the Post Office Department in Washington, D.C., but "her habit of coming and going as she pleased made her 'a hindrance to other clerks'."[1] She was reduced to the lowest-grade clerk and later resigned. She soon became destitute. "When poverty came on . . . , she bore it in silence, with all the pride of a Southern woman, until it became unsupportable," and she had to depend on money sent by Northern friends. Never forgiven by Richmonders, she died at the age of 88 in 1900 and was buried in Shockoe Cemetery.[2]

EMMIE CRUMP married William B. Lightfoot. An account she kept in her diary was published in 1933 under the title, "The Evacuation of Richmond," in *The Virginia Magazine of History and Biography*, Virginia Historical Society. KATE MASON ROWLAND, a grand-niece of James Mason, contributed articles on the Confederacy throughout her life to various publications. She never married and died at the age of 77 in Richmond, where she spent her last 12 years. JUDITH W. BROKENBROUGH MCGUIRE lived with husband, John, at "Westwood," on the Pamunkey River about 30 miles east of Richmond. In addition to her book on Richmond, *Diary of a Southern Refugee During the War*, she also wrote *General Robert E. Lee, the Christian Soldier* in 1873. She died in 1897 and was buried in her native town of Tappahannock, Virginia.

ABRAHAM LINCOLN returned to Washington, D.C., after his Richmond inspection. Ten days later, while attending a play at Ford's Theater, he was shot by John Wilkes Booth and died the following morning. The president's death proved a great tragedy for the South. Historians believe that had he lived, the South would have recovered more rapidly, and, perhaps, made an easier transition to the acceptance of the rights of all men to be free.

ROBERT E. LEE accepted the post of president of Washington College in Lexington, Virginia, five months after the war ended. The college was later renamed Washington and Lee University. In that post he worked to rebuild the South through education. After a brief visit with friends in Richmond in 1870, Lee left the former Confederate capital for the last time on May 26, and "passed from the central stage of his life's drama as though he had been the humblest actor. . . . " The general died of a stroke at his Lexington home five months later. MARY CUSTIS LEE outlived her husband by three years.

VARINA DAVIS met up with her husband May 9, 1865, and was captured with him a day later at Irwinsville, Georgia. She was released and worked for her husband's freedom during the two years of his imprisonment. After he died, she continued to live at "Beauvoir" until her death in 1906. She recorded her memoirs of the war years in a two-volume book, *Jefferson Davis, Ex-President of the Confederate States of America: A Memoir*. It was published in 1890.

JEFFERSON DAVIS, who held onto the belief that the South would win, tried to keep his government together until the end. He was captured a little more than a month after he left Richmond. He was imprisoned for two years at Fort Monroe in Hampton, Virginia, confined much of the time to a small cell with 24-hour guards inside and outside. He was never brought to trial and was finally released May 13, 1867.

After a period of recovery from poor health, Davis traveled through Europe with his wife, Varina. Upon his return he unsuccessfully tried several business ventures. In his early 70s, he and Mrs. Davis retired to "Beauvoir," a Mississippi home on the Gulf of Mexico given to the couple by Mrs. Sarah A. Dorsey, a family friend. There he wrote his memoirs in a book entitled *The Rise and Fall of the Confederate Government*. The ex-Confederate president died in New Orleans at the age of 82. His body was brought to Richmond four years later for reburial in Hollywood Cemetery.

E N D N O T E S

Chapter 1

1. John Beauchamp Jones, *A Rebel War Clerk's Diary at the Confederate States Capital*, p. 464.
2. A dramatization based on those who witnessed the service, including: Mrs. William B. Lightfoot, "The Evacuation of Richmond"; Edward A. Pollard, *Southern History of the War*; Dallas Tucker, "The Fall of Richmond."
3. Clifford Dowdey, *The Wartime Papers of R. E. Lee*, pp. 925–926.
4. Dallas Tucker, "The Fall of Richmond," p. 152.
5. Harrison Peyton, *Moses Drury Hoge*, pp. 290–291.
6. Ibid., p. 290.
7. Ibid., p. 492.
8. Judith W. Brokenbrough McGuire, *Diary of a Southern Refugee During the War*, pp. 343–344.
9. Richard S. Ewell, "Evacuation of Richmond," pp. 247–252.
10. Ibid.
11. Phoebe Yates Pember, *A Southern Woman's Story*, pp. 37–46.
12. John Leyburn, "The Fall of Richmond," pp. 92–97.
13. Ibid.
14. Virginia E. Dare, *One Woman in the War*, pp. 94–96.
15. Mrs. Roger A. Pryor, *Reminiscences of Peace and War*, pp. 354–355.

Chapter 2

1. Varina Howell Davis, *Jefferson Davis, Ex-President of the Confederate States of America*, p. 191.
2. The exact look of the room is not known. The description is based on how the Museum of Confederacy researchers believed the room looked.
3. Mary Boykin Miller Chesnut, *A Diary from Dixie*, p. 305.
4. Thomas Cooper DeLeon, *Four Years in Rebel Capitals*, p. 155.
5. W. F. Spencer, "A French View of the Fall of Richmond," p. 181.
6. Ibid.
7. Raphael Semmes, *The Confederate Raider Alabama*, p. 420.
8. Ibid.
9. Richard M. Lee, *General Lee's City*, p. 115.
10. Mrs. William B. Lightfoot, "The Evacuation of Richmond," p. 216.
11. "Records [Richmond] Common Council, Nos. 1–21, 1782–1883," Reel No. 15, Virginia State Library and Archives.
12. Ibid.
13. Phoebe Yates Pember, *A Southern Woman's Story*, p. 164.
14. Ibid., p. 168.

15. Elizabeth Van Lew Papers. The original papers are stored at the New York Public Library. The page numbers have been changed several times and thus are not listed here.
16. George Putnam, *A Prisoner of War in Virginia*, pp. 278–279; Goss, Warren Lee, *A Soldier's Story of His Captivity at Andersonville, Belle Isle, and Other Rebel Prisons*, pp. 33–34.
17. Edward A. Pollard, *Southern History of the War*, pp. 495–496.

Chapter 3

1. John Beauchamp Jones, *A Rebel War Clerk's Diary of the Confederate States Capital*, p. 466.
2. William H. Parker, *Recollections of A Naval Officer*, pp. 349–351.
3. "Records [Richmond] Common Council, Nos. 1–21, 1782–1883," Reel No. 15, Virginia State Library and Archives.
4. Clifford Dowdey, *The Wartime Papers of R. E. Lee*, p. 927.
5. Van Lew Papers.
6. Jefferson Davis Letters, Museum of the Confederacy.
7. William H. Parker, *Recollections of A Naval Officer*, pp. 349–351.
8. Raphael Semmes, *The Confederate Raider Alabama*, pp. 420–426.
9. Jones, p. 196.
10. John Leyburn, "The Fall of Richmond," pp. 92–97.
11. Ibid., p. 146.
12. Mary Boykin Miller Chesnut, *Dixie After the War*, p. 35.
13. Hudson Strode, *Jefferson Davis*, p. 170.
14. Thomas Cooper DeLeon, *Four Years in Rebel Capitals*, p. 395.
15. Walter H. Taylor, *General Lee, His Campaigns in Virginia*, p. 276.
16. Lilian M. Cook, "Girl Describes Evacuation," *Richmond News Leader*, pp. 1–2.

Chapter 4

1. John Beauchamp Jones, *A Rebel War Clerk's Diary of the Confederate States Capital*, p. 467.
2. Sallie Ann Brock Putnam, *Richmond During the War*, p. 365.
3. G. Powell Hill, "First Burial of General Hill's Remains," pp. 183–186.
4. Constance Cary Harrison, *Recollections Grave and Gay*. This dramatization was based on these recollections.
5. G. Powell Hill, "First Burial of General Hill's Remains," pp. 183–185.
6. Edward H. Ripley, *The Capture and Occupation of Richmond, April 3, 1865*, pp. 73–76.
7. Phoebe Yates Pember, *A Southern Woman's Story*, pp. 11–92.
8. "Records [Richmond] Common Council, Nos. 1–21, 1782–1883," Reel No. 15, Virginia State Library and Archives.
9. Author's dramatization based on the following sources: Edward A. Pollard, *Southern History of the War*; Mary Boykin Miller Chesnut, *Dixie After the War*.
10. Chesnut, p. 15.

Chapter 5

1. Mrs. William B. Lightfoot, "The Evacuation of Richmond," pp. 215–222.
2. Kathleen Bruce, *Virginia Iron Manufacture in the Slave Era*, pp. 179–231.
3. Clement Sulivane, "The Evacuation," pp. 725–726.
4. Phoebe Yates Pember, *A Southern Woman's Story*, p. 133.
5. Godfrey Weitzel, *Richmond Occupied*, p. 10.
6. Ibid., p. 10.
7. Thomas Morris Chester, *Thomas Morris Chester, Black Civil War Correspondent*, pp. 288–289.
8. Godfrey Weitzel, *Richmond Occupied*, p. 52.
9. Raphael Semmes, *The Confederate Raider Alabama*, pp. 420–426.
10. Hubbard Taylor Minor, "Diary of Hubbard Taylor Minor, Jr.," p. 35.
11. John Beauchamp Jones, *A Rebel War Clerk's Diary of the Confederate States Capital*, p. 467.
12. Thomas Cooper DeLeon, *Four Years in Rebel Capitals*, p. 149.
13. Ibid.; Richard M. Lee, *General Lee's City*, pp. 134–135.
14. G. Powell Hill, "First Burial of General Hill's Remains," pp. 183–186.

Chapter 6

1. Van Lew Papers. (None of the official records or accounts mention Miss Van Lew's flag being seen by the Union soldiers entering Richmond April 3, 1865, although it is possible hers was the first United States flag flown that day.)
2. Ibid.
3. Henry B. Dawson, *The First Flag Over Richmond, Virginia, April 3, 1865*. The colors of the Fourth Massachusetts Cavalry were placed on the roof.
4. Mrs. William B. Lightfoot, "The Evacuation of Richmond," pp. 215–21.
5. Myrta Lockett Avary, *A Virginia Girl in the Civil War*, p. 364.
6. Edward A. Pollard, *A New Southern History of the War of the Confederates*, pp. 692–696.
7. Thomas Morris Chester, *Thomas Morris Chester, Black Civil War Correspondent*, pp. 291–292.
8. Ibid.
9. Godfrey Weitzel, *Richmond Occupied*, p. 54.
10. Judith W. Brokenbrough McGuire, *Diary of a Southern Refugee During the War*, pp. 345–346.
11. Mary Boykin Miller Chesnut, *Dixie After the War*, p. 11.
12. Lilian M. Cook's "Girl Describes Evacuation," *Richmond News Leader*, p. 2.

Chapter 7

1. Godfrey Weitzel, *Richmond Occupied*, p. 10.
2. Based on Library of Congress photographs.

3. Kathleen Bruce, *Virginia Iron Manufacture in the Slave Era*, pp. 179–231.
4. Edward A. Pollard, *Southern History of the War*, p. 495.
5. New York *Tribune*, April 4, 1865.
6. Thomas Cooper DeLeon, *Four Years in Rebel Capitals*, p. 361.
7. "The Evacuation of Richmond by the Confederate Army," *Richmond Whig*, p. 1.

Chapter 8

1. Edward A. Pollard, *Southern History of the War*, p. 497.
2. Mrs. William B. Lightfoot, "The Evacuation of Richmond," p. 219.
3. Phoebe Yates Pember, *A Southern Woman's Story*, pp. 139–145.
4. Judith W. Brokenbrough McGuire, *Diary of a Southern Refugee During the War*, pp. 346–348.
5. Myrta Lockett Avary, *A Virginia Girl in the Civil War*, pp. 365–367.
6. Faith Morris, Interviewer, "Interviews with Virginia Ex-Slaves."
7. Judith W. Brokenbrough McGuire, *Diary of a Southern Refugee During the War*, p. 349.
8. Constance Cary Harrison, *Recollections Grave and Gay*, pp. 210–216.
9. Kate Mason Rowland Papers, Museum of the Confederacy.
10. Author's dramatization based on Godfrey Weitzel, *Richmond Occupied*.
11. Mrs. William B. Lightfoot, "The Evacuation of Richmond," p. 220.
12. Wyndham B. Blanton, *The Making of a Downtown Church*, p. 295.
13. Lilian M. Cook, "Cook's Diary," p. 2.
14. Elizabeth Van Lew Papers.
15. Phoebe Yates Pember, *A Southern Woman's Story*, pp. 139–140.

Chapter 9

1. Godfrey Weitzel, *Richmond Occupied*, p. 55.
2. Phoebe Yates Pember, *A Southern Woman's Story*, pp. 11–192.
3. Jennie D. Harrold, "Reminiscences of Richmond 1861–1865," Museum of the Confederacy.
4. Donald C. Pfanz, *The Petersburg Campaign*, pp. 58–68; Gustavua A. Myers, "Abraham Lincoln in Richmond," pp. 319–321.
5. Mrs. Roger A. Pryor, *Reminiscences of Peace and War*, p. 357.
6. Gustavua A. Myers, "Abraham Lincoln in Richmond," pp. 319–326.
7. Ibid.
8. Thomas Morris Chester, *Thomas Morris Chester, Black Civil War Correspondent*, p. 295.
9. Ibid.
10. David Dixon Porter, *Incidents and Anecdotes of the Civil War*, pp. 279–298.
11. Mrs. William B. Lightfoot, "The Evacuation of Richmond," pp. 215–222.
12. Judith W. Brokenbrough McGuire, *Diary of a Southern Refugee During the War*, p. 350.
13. Thomas Morris Chester, *Thomas Morris Chester, Black Civil War Correspondent*, p. 295–296.

14. Gustavua A. Myers, "Abraham Lincoln in Richmond," pp. 319–321.
15. Thomas Morris Chester, *Thomas Morris Chester, Black Civil War Correspondent*, p. 295.
16. Thomas Thatcher Graves, "The Occupation," p. 278.

Chapter 10

1. Thomas Cooper DeLeon, *Four Years in Rebel Capitals*, p. 402.
2. George Gary Eggleston, *A Rebel's Recollections*; Clifford Dowdey, *The Wartime Papers of R. E. Lee*, p. 549.
3. Walter H. Taylor, *General Lee*, p. 281; John S. Barnes, "With Lincoln From Washington to Richmond in 1865," pp. 515–524; Thomas Thatcher Graves, "The Occupation," p. 728.
4. Ibid. (Researchers debate whether Davis's office was on the first or second floor of the presidential mansion.)
5. John A. Campbell, *Recollections of the Evacuation of Richmond, April 2d, 1865*, p. 8.
6. Author's dramatization.
7. "Last Days of the Southern Confederacy," pp. 329–333.
8. John A. Campbell, *Recollections of the Evacuation of Richmond*, pp. 3–17.
9. Sallie Ann Brock Putnam, *Richmond During the War*, p. 372.
10. Thomas Morris Chester, *Thomas Morris Chester, Black Civil War Correspondent*, p. 297.
11. Godfrey Weitzel, *Richmond Occupied*, p. 56.
12. Thomas Cooper DeLeon, *Four Years in Rebel Capitals*, pp. 364–365.
13. Myrta Lockett Avary, *A Virginia Girl in the Civil War*, pp. 370–372.

Chapter 11

1. Thomas Cooper DeLeon, *Four Years in Rebel Capitals*, p. 367.
2. Ibid., p. 367; Author's dramatization based on accounts of Lee's return to Richmond.

Epilogue

1. Richard P. Weinert, "Federal Spies in Richmond," pp. 28–34.
2. "Grant's Woman Spy," *Boston Sunday Herald*, p. 1.

BIBLIOGRAPHY

Primary Sources
Books

Avary, Myrta Lockett. *A Virginia Girl in the Civil War*. New York: Appleton & Co., 1903.

Blanton, Wyndham B. *The Making of a Downtown Church. The History of the Second Presbyterian Church, Richmond, Va. 1845–1945*. Richmond: John Knox Press, 1945.

Bruce, Kathleen. *Virginia Iron Manufacture in the Slave Era*. New York: A. M. Kelly, 1968.

Campbell, John A. *Recollections of the Evacuation of Richmond, April 2d, 1865*. Baltimore: John Murphy & Co., 1890.

Chesnut, Mary Boykin Miller. *A Diary from Dixie*. Edited by Isabella D. Martin and Myrta Lockett Avary. New York: Appleton & Co., 1905.

Chester, Thomas Morris. *Thomas Morris Chester, Black Civil War Correspondent: His Dispatches from the Virginia Front*. Edited by R. J. M. Blackett. Baton Rouge: Louisiana State University Press, 1989.

Dare, Virginia E. *One Woman in the War*. Charleston, S.C.: News & Courier Book Press, 1885.

Davis, Jefferson. *The Rise and Fall of the Confederate Government*. Vol. 2. New York: D. Appleton, 1881.

Davis, Varina Howell. *Jefferson Davis, Ex-President of the Confederate States of America: A Memoir of His Wife*. Vol. 1. New York: Bedford Co., 1890.

Dawson, Henry B. *The First Flag Over Richmond, Virginia, April 3, 1865*. Morrisiana, N.Y.: Privately printed, 1865.

DeLeon, Thomas Cooper. *Four Years in Rebel Capitals*. New York: Crowell Collier Publishing Co., 1962.

Dowdey, Clifford. *The Wartime Papers of R. E. Lee*. New York: Bramhell House, 1961.

Eggleston, George Gary. *A Rebel's Recollections*. New York: G. P. Putnam & Sons, 1878.

Goss, Warren Lee. *A Soldier's Story of His Captivity at Andersonville, Belle Isle, and Other Rebel Prisons*. Boston: Richardson Co., 1871.

Harrison, Constance Cary. *Recollections Grave and Gay*. New York: Charles Scribner & Sons, 1911.

Harrison, Peyton. *Moses Drury Hoge: Life and Letters*. Richmond: Presbyterian Committee of Publications, 1899.

Jones, John Beauchamp. *A Rebel War Clerk's Diary at the Confederate States Capital*. Vol. 2. New York: Old Hickory Bookshop, 1935.

Lee, Richard M. *General Lee's City*. McLean, Va.: EPM Publications, Inc., 1987.

McGuire, Judith White Brokenbrough. *Diary of a Southern Refugee During the War by a Lady of Virginia.* New York: E. J. Hale & Son, 1867.

Parker, William Harwar. *Recollections of a Naval Officer.* New York: Charles Scribner's Sons, 1883.

Pember, Phoebe Yates. *A Southern Woman's Story.* New York: G. W. Carelton & Co., 1879.

Pfanz, Donald C. *The Petersburg Campaign. Abraham Lincoln at City Point, March 20–April 9, 1865.* Lynchburg, Va.: H.E. Howard, Inc., 1989.

Pollard, Edward A. *Southern History of the War.* New York: Charles B. Richardson, 1866.

——*Life of Jefferson Davis, with a secret history of the Southern Confederacy gathered "Behind the Scenes in Richmond,"* 1869. (Reprint 1969 Books for Libraries Press, Freeport, New York.)

——*The Lost Cause: A New Southern History of the War of the Confederates.* New York: E. B. Treat & Co. 1866.

Porter, David Dixon. *Incidents and Anecdotes of the Civil War.* New York: D. Appleton and Company, 1885.

Pryor, Mrs. Roger A. *Reminiscences of Peace and War.* New York: MacMillan, 1924.

Putnam, George. *A Prisoner of War in Virginia 1864–5.* New York: G. P. Putnam & Sons. 1912.

Putnam, Sallie Ann Brock. *Richmond During the War: Four Years of Personal Observations by a Richmond Lady.* New York: G. W. Carleton & Co., 1867.

Ripley, Edward H. *The Capture and Occupation of Richmond, April 3, 1865.* New York: G. P. Putnam & Sons, 1907.

Ryan, David D. *Lewis Ginter's Richmond.* Richmond: Whittet & Shepperson, 1991.

Sandburg, Carl. *Abraham Lincoln. The War Years.* Vol. 4. New York: Harcourt, Brace & World, 1939.

Semmes, Raphael. *The Confederate Raider Alabama.* Cape Town Amsterdam: A. A. Balkema, 1958.

Strode, Hudson. *Jefferson Davis. Tragic Hero.* Vol. 3. New York: Harcourt, Brace & World, Inc., 1964.

Taylor, Walter H. *General Lee, His Campaigns in Virginia.* Norfolk: Nusbaum Book & News Co., 1906.

Weitzel, Godfrey. *Richmond Occupied.* Edited by Louis H. Manarin. Official Publication Number 16. Richmond: Richmond Civil War Centennial Commission, 1965.

Primary Sources

Letters, Articles, Etc.

Barnes, John S. "With Lincoln From Washington to Richmond in 1865." *Appleton's Magazine,* June 1907, pp. 515–524.

Cook, Lilian M. "Girl Describes Evacuation." *Richmond News Leader,* April 3, 1935, pp. 1–2.

"Diary of Hubbard Taylor Minor, Jr." *Civil War Times Illustrated*, December 1974, p. 35.

Ewell, Richard S. "Evacuation of Richmond." *Southern Historical Society Papers*, Vol 13, pp. 247–252.

"Grant's Woman Spy." *Boston Sunday Herald*, Nov. 14, 1900, p. 1.

Graves, Thomas Thatcher. "The Occupation." *Battles and Leaders*, Vol. 4, p. 728.

Harrison, Constance C. "A Virginia Girl in the First Year of the War." *The Century Illustrated Monthly Magazine*, August 1885, pp. 606–614.

Hill, G. Powell. "First Burial of General Hill's Remains." *Southern Historical Society Papers*, Vol. 19, pp. 183–186.

"Interviews of Virginia Ex-Slaves," Faith Morris, Interviewer, Virginia State Library and Archives, 1937.

"Jefferson Davis Letters," Eleanor S. Brockenbrough Library, The Museum of the Confederacy, Richmond, Virginia.

"Kate Mason Rowland Letters," Eleanor S. Brockenbrough Library, The Museum of the Confederacy, Richmond, Virginia.

"Last Days of the Southern Confederacy." *Southern Historical Society Papers*, Vol. 19, pp. 329–333.

Leyburn, John. "The Fall of Richmond." *Harper's New Monthly Magazine*, April 1866, pp. 92–97.

Lightfoot, Mrs. William B. "The Evacuation of Richmond." *The Virginia Magazine of History and Biography*, January 1933, pp. 215–222.

Morris, Faith, Interviewer. "Interviews of Virginia Ex-Slaves." Virginia State Library and Achives, 1932.

Myers, Gustavua A. "Abraham Lincoln in Richmond." *The Virginia Magazine of History and Biography*, October 1933, pp. 319–321.

New York Tribune, April 4, 1865.

"Records [Richmond] Common Council, Nos. 1–21, 1782–1883," Reel No. 15, Virginia State Library and Archives.

"Reminiscences of Richmond from 1861–1865," Jennie D. Harrold Papers, Eleanor S. Brockenbrough Library, The Museum of the Confederacy.

Richmond. Virginia Historical Society. Letters, military passes and miscellaneous papers collected by Elizabeth Van Lew Album.

Spencer, W. F. "A French View of the Fall of Richmond: Alfred's Paul's Report to Drouyn de Llys, April 11, 1865." *The Virginia Magazine of History and Biography*, April 1965, pp. 178–188.

Sulivane, Clement. "The Evacuation." *Battles and Leaders of the Civil War*, Vol. 4, pp. 725–726. New York: The Century Company, 1887.

"The Evacuation of Richmond by the Confederate Army." *Richmond Whig*, April 3, 1865, p. 1.

Tucker, Dallas. "The Fall of Richmond." *The Virginia Magazine of History and Biography*, Vol. 29, p. 152.

Weinert, Richard P. "Federal Spies in Richmond." *Civil War Times Illustrated*, February 1965, pp. 28–34.

General Background

Books

Before Freedom Came. African-American Life in the Antebellum South. Richmond: The Museum of the Confederacy and The University Press of Virginia, 1991.

Bill, Alfred Hoyt. *The Beleaguered City, Richmond 1861–1865.* New York: Alfred A. Knopf, 1946.

Boykin, E. M. *The Falling Flag—Evacuation of Richmond. Retreat and Surrender at Appomattox.* New York: E. J. Hale & Son, 1874.

Brewer, James H. *The Confederate Negro: Virginia's Craftsmen and Military Laborers, 1861–1865.* Durham: Duke University Press, 1969.

Cavada, Frederic F. *Libby Life, Experiences of a Prisoner of War in Richmond, Va.* Philadelphia: J. B. Lippencott & Co., 1865.

Chesterman, William D. *Guide to Richmond and the Battle-fields.* Richmond: J. L. Hill Printing Co., 1894.

Christian, W. Asbury. *Richmond Her Past and Present.* Richmond: L. H. Jenkins Co., 1912.

Coulter, E. Merton. *The Confederate States of America, 1861–1865.* Vol 7, *A History of the South.* Baton Rouge, Louisiana State University Press, 1950.

Dabney, Virginius. *Richmond: The Story of a City.* Garden City, N.Y.: Doubleday & Co., 1976.

——*Virginia, The New Dominion.* Garden City, N.Y.: Doubleday & Co., 1971.

Davis, Burke. *To Appomattox; Nine Days in April 1865.* New York: Rinehart & Co., 1959.

DeLeon, Thomas Cooper. *Belles, Beaux and Brains of the 60's.* New York: G. W. Dillingham Co., 1909.

Dew, Charles B. *Ironmaker to the Confederacy. Joseph B. Anderson and the Tredegar Iron Works.* New Haven: Yale University Press, 1966.

Dowdey, Clifford. *Experiment in Rebellion.* Freeport, N.Y.: Books for Libraries Press, 1904.

——*Lee.* Boston: Little Brown and Company, 1965.

Duke, Maurice, and Jordan, Daniel P. *A Richmond Reader 1733–1983.* Chapel Hill, N.C.: The University of North Carolina Press, 1983.

Freeman, Douglas S. *R. E. Lee, a Biography.* 4 Vols. New York: Charles Scribner's Sons, 1934–1935.

Hoehling, A.A., and Mary. *The Day Richmond Died.* New York: A.S. Barnes & Co., 1981.

Jones, Katherine M. *Ladies of Richmond, Confederate Capital.* New York: Bobbs Merrill Co., 1962.

Kane, Harnett T. *Spies for the Blue and Gray.* New York: Hanover House, 1954.

Kimmel, Stanley P. *Mr. Davis' Richmond.* New York: Coward-McCann, 1958.

McCarthy, C. *Walks About Richmond.* Richmond: McCarthy & Ellyson, 1870.

McPherson, James M. *The Negro's Civil War.* New York: Pantheon Books, 1961.

Patrick, Rembert W. *The Fall of Richmond.* Baton Rouge, La.: Louisiana State University Press, 1961.

Sanders, E. W., and Bowers, C. W. *Illustrated Richmond.* Richmond: Richmond News Co., 1908.

Scott, Mary Wingfield. *Houses of Old Richmond.* Richmond: The Valentine Museum, 1941.

Semmes, Raphael. *Memoirs of Service Afloat.* Baltimore: Kelley & Co., 1869.

Stanard, Mary Newton. *Richmond, Its People and Its Story.* Philadelphia: J. B. Lippincott Co., 1923.

Thomas, Emory M. *The Confederate State of Richmond; A Biography of the Capital.* Austin: University of Texas Press, 1991.

Weddell, Elizabeth W. *St. Paul's Church, Richmond, Virginia, Its Historical Years and Memories.* Richmond: The William Byrd Press, 1931.

General Background

Letters, Articles, Etc.

Bailey, John H. "Crazy Bet, Union Spy." *Virginia Cavalcade,* Spring, 1952, pp. 14–17.

Gorgas, Amelia. "As I Saw It—One Woman's Account of the Fall of Richmond." *Civil War Times Illustrated,* May 1986, pp. 40–43.

"Images of Which History Was Made Bore the Mathew Brady Labels." *Smithsonian,* July 1977, pp. 24–34.

Langston, Loomis J. "The First Federal to Enter Richmond." *Richmond Dispatch,* February 10, 1893.

"The Richmond Campaign." War of Rebellion. Official Records of the Union and Confederate Armies. Series 1, Vol. 46 (Parts 1–3). Washington: National Archives, U.S. Government Printing Office, 1894–1895.

Weathers, Willie T. "Judith W. McGuire. A Lady of Richmond." *The Virginia Magazine of History and Biography,* pp. 100–113.

INDEX

BIOGRAPHICAL NOTE

DAVID D. RYAN is a Richmond native and a graduate of the University of Richmond. For 20 years a reporter and photographer for the *Richmond Times-Dispatch*, he now devotes his time to historic research and writing. Among his four books on Virginia history are *The Falls of the James, Gwynn's Island, Va.*, and *Lewis Ginter's Richmond*. Mr. Ryan is also the writer and illustrator of a series of collectable cards on the Civil War.